Winning Against All Odds

Leave the Past Behind
Turn Failure Into Opportunity
Equip Yourself for Success

By
Dr. Donald Shorter

Harrison House
Tulsa, Oklahoma

12 11 10 09 08   10 9 8 7 6 5 4 3 2 1

Winning Against All Odds:
Leave the Past Behind, Turn Failure Into Opportunity, Equip Yourself for Success
ISBN 13: 978-1-57794-848-3
ISBN 10: 1-57794-848-3
Copyright © 2008 by Dr. Donald Shorter
P.O. Box 44800
Tacoma, WA 98448
www.pacificchristiancenter.org

Published by Harrison House Publishers
P.O. Box 35035
Tulsa, Oklahoma 74153
www.harrisonhouse.com

Contents

Introduction

I n the heart of every human being is a desire to be a winner, but some people pay a high price to try to win in life. Why do you think we are seeing such a gambling phenomena in our cities and other regions of our country, on the Web, and around the world? Gambling has become such an important industry to so many people that to some it doesn't matter what kind of gambling it is—they'll just play it to win.

Yet winning at any cost is not truly winning in life.

The strong desire to be a winner is a God-given desire that is in every one of us right now (even children). Whether it is the Super Bowl, the World Series, World Cup Soccer, the musical charts, the NBA, a spelling bee contest, or anything else we do in life, people want to be number one, not number 13 or 17 or in third place or even second place.

I'm here to tell you that *there is nothing wrong with being a winner.* It's trying to become a winner at any cost that is not success.

You may win the game and receive material possessions like money, a trophy, or a medal, but not truly win in life. To truly win in this life you will have to fight the good fight of faith, believing that you should win and can win against any opposing forces that would try to come against you. That is what this book is designed to help you do.

I believe that by the time you finish reading this message you will be completely equipped on how to position yourself to be able to win against all odds—and I really do mean *win against all odds!*

This process can begin right now by making a simple final decision in your mind that winning is okay. It is all right to want to win. It's all right to want to have a winning life or lifestyle. It's all right to want to be around winners and not losers. Relax, it's okay; it doesn't make you a bad person because you are tired of losing or tired of being at the end of everything or overlooked or even forgotten.

It's all right to know that you can win in your finances, that you can have an award-winning family or a winning marriage or a successful single life. It's all right to believe that you can be chosen and not overlooked, and to know that you are special. See, I believe that God wants you to win in all areas. He wants you to know that you are a winner and you can win, even if the odds are stacked against you.

The truth is, when you finish this book and start to put these principles into action, it won't matter what the odds are against you!

I know this sounds too good to be true, but it is true, and it's good. Any opposition should not be a stopping point for you, but rather a stepping-stone for progress. The word *hindrance* is a synonym to the word *opposition;* it is anything that gets in the way. But hindrances are not a problem once you apply God's winning principles to your life.

In these pages you are going to learn how to remove unnecessary things from your way by just simply making changes and adjustments to the most important area in your life—your thoughts. You will learn how to think as a winner as well as how to talk as a winner, how to believe as a winner, how to use the Word as a winner, and how to live as a winner—because you are a winner!

I know what I am telling you—you are a winner!

How can I say something like that so boldly? I believe in patterning my own life only after successful principles, so the winning ways I'll be sharing with you have worked for me—and if they can work for me, they can work for you.

I am also a pilot, and when I was learning how to fly, one thing for sure was that I didn't want to take lessons from another pilot who was crashing his airplane every other weekend. I know that I'm being dramatic here, but I want you to get the point. I wanted to learn from a pilot who had more successful flights then bad ones.

Winning is a matter of learning how to model yourself after winners to the point where you will know that you are patterning yourself as a winner on purpose. When you are patterning yourself after a positive position like that to become a winner, you don't mind making changes.

I believe that you are ready to make all the needed changes to become a winner because you chose to read this book. The process has been started for you at this very moment, so feel good about the choice you have already made today. As we go through the winning process together, keep in mind that I will honestly tell you what works beginning with only this: Know that changes are good, and positive changes will take you closer and closer to being the winner that you desire to be.

Changes can become a lifestyle for you beginning right now. So before you continue to read, I want you to make your first change and get fired up to win by declaring the end from the beginning—start saying that you are a winner.

CHAPTER 1

A New Outlook on Life

You were created by God to win. Yet when it comes to winning in life, so many people think of it as a process of chance. Chance says that things are not always consistent in the process of receiving this way. Chance, luck, happenstance are all very uncertain in their origin because they lend themselves to no real solid, unmovable basis for guaranteed success. This is not how to truly win in life God's way.

I feel I can speak on this subject because from my childhood up I have firsthand experience with chance and what it can do to lives. You see, at the age of seven I was introduced to the effects of chance running a person's life through gambling.

A close family member was invited to go to one evening of gambling that started at 7 P.M. and ran until 9:30 each night. A person participating in this type of gambling would have to miss certain things in order to be there. This particular evening they were prepared to spend the night gambling with the innocent game called bingo. You may chuckle at this, but it turned out to be nearly 40 years of bondage and gambling addiction for this person, always waiting to see if she could win by chance.

That first evening my close relative went just to see how it works, and lo and behold, she won $700—just enough to get excited (in 1962). From that point on, the game of chance was on for her.

This was a very domesticated person, a woman who stayed home and always took great care of her six children while her military husband was deployed around the world. She was always so caring for others, and don't get me wrong; she continued to be a caring, loving, person, and to me, as you have probably guessed, a great mother.

My mother got so hooked on winning by fate, chance, luck, or without being jinxed that soon she was going to play bingo morning, noon, and night to feed this addiction of being a winner. The consequences in a situation like this are never good for those involved, and for my mother they continued virtually daily for nearly 40 years. *Chance* was the motivating factor—"I may win big tonight; the jackpot is this amount."

Over all those many years our lifestyle changed, all because of her winning $700 at the beginning. For one thing, to not see my mother night after night, and many times all day after the age of seven, was a high price for me to pay. I did not like it at all. She had new priorities that rearranged our entire lives, all revolving around the chance to win big that day. Chance took my mother away from me, and she simply could not be there at those times of the day and night. For a seven-year-old, that can be, and was for me, a devastating blow. I had to share her with the bingo parlor.

This was not a job—she had to pay and pay and pay to play the game of chance; and it was not cheap, on a military income, to keep this addiction going. So it became a drain on the family income. Sure, she would win more than that once in the nearly 40 years of chance, but it was always too little too late, and only enough to keep chance alive.

It meant so many other challenges too. For one thing it was new responsibilities for me of taking care of my brother and sister because my mom acted as though this was her job, and we knew she would not be home until 10:30 each night after bingo. The children and even the entire family would often sit at home and wait to find out if she had won to see if we were going to be able to have extra money for certain things.

Chance also began to give us kids some promises like "If I win, I will buy you a new bike," or something else new, "so stay home and be good 'for chance.'"

From a personal standpoint, I would say that chance is no way for anyone to live their lives, because chance leaves too much—to chance. The problem is that sometimes, by chance, you do get a temporary victory. But through many evil spiritual forces (which we'll discuss later on), these wins are simply tokens to bondage. It is like a new drug user looking for a high and having a "good high." The person continues to chance it again and again until they are either hooked, overdosed, or strung out on the same drug that they thought they were mastering.

Chance is not how the God of the universe operates.

God is our Source of true winning and real success, and He says, "Trust in the Lord with all your heart and lean not on your own understanding; in all your ways acknowledge him, and *he* will make your paths straight. Do not be wise in your own eyes; fear the Lord [or revere, honor, respect Him] and shun evil" (Prov. 3:5-7 NIV). Yet many times people from various walks of life like athletes, actors and actresses, corporate executives, business owners, and sometimes even ministers deal with this common problem of trusting in someone or something other than God for success.

With athletes, for example, this problem crops up in their quest to be number one on the stat sheets. That is true for people in the entertainment industry, like movies and radio broadcasting, too. I know this from personal experience, as we'll see in a moment.

I believe it is important to make sure that in your quest for winning you seek first God, and He will become your Source of victory. He is the anchor of our testimony of why we have success.

As He Is, So Are You

You are one of a kind. God created you that way. No other person has your fingerprint; no one has your DNA. You are unique, you are an original. No one else will be able to do exactly like you what you were born to do, because there is only one you. So there is no need to copycat someone else; God will work through you, using the talents He has given you, if you trust in Him. You are on the stage of life, not performing for man but fulfilling your God-given purpose in life.

Yet we are told in Hebrews 6:12 to imitate (but not try to be that person) who "through faith and patience inherit the promises." Simply put, this is saying that you should follow those who are winning and find out how you should live in this world. Our most sought-out example should be the one that was given to us over two thousand years ago.

Jesus Christ was obedient until His death on the cross, but He is no longer on the cross. He is at the right hand of God in heaven, ruling and reigning and praying for us (Heb. 12:2), and the way He is *now* should be the way you see yourself. He is victorious, so you have the right to see yourself as victorious—not under the circumstances of life but on top and rising—because "as He is, so are you in this world" (1 John 4:17).

When I say "He" in that verse, I'm talking about God who created the universe—the awesome God who created you—which means I'm talking about Jesus, who was "not merely God-like, but in the fullest sense, God."[1] So, how is He?

Two thousand years ago Jesus was beaten and then nailed on the cross and suffered in our place. Yes, He suffered and yielded His will to His Father's will for us, but that is not how He is *now,* that's how He *was.* He has risen from the grave and sits with His Father in His throne. (See Rev. 3:21.) Why then are there so many photos and necklaces depicting Jesus still on the cross, yet I haven't seen in a photo or on a necklace the victorious side of Jesus displayed as seated on the throne?

We should depict Jesus as He is *now;* then the image we portray of Him will depict a life of winning.

When you are following a leader, that person is in front because they have already been there and done that, and now they can coach you along. God is your leader when you become born again, and He sent His Son Jesus to set the pattern to establish the best course of action to take to win in life because Jesus was tested and passed the test.

We do not have a High Priest who cannot sympathize with our weak-nesses, but was in all points tempted as we are, yet without sin. Let

us therefore come boldly to the throne of grace, that we may obtain
mercy and find grace to help in time of need.

Hebrews 4:15-16

If Jesus had lost, you would have had to stay in a losing position. But He won the battle, and you are a winner because of it!
That's why whatever He is, so are you. If He was broke in heaven
(can you imagine a God who was broke?), for instance, then you
should be broke. Before you can be broke, God has to become
broke and destitute first, but since He is not broke, then you are
(present tense) not broke.

Now don't go look at your checkbook and say that I am lying.
Maybe in the natural you don't have much, but that's not who you
are. If you desire to live as a winner, you must think like one first,
and you must think that you are a winner *now.* We're going to take
an in-depth look at our thought life later on, but let me give you
an example.

One time my wife, Kathy, and I bought a run-down, ugly, dirty
old house. We had just started investing in real estate and bought
this house for only $500. Family members and friends thought we
were crazy, and in the natural, we looked crazy because we
decided to live in the house. But to us this house was valuable
because we could see its potential. It had a lot of character to us,
a nice fixer-upper.

We could see past the mounds of trash in the front yard, the
dirty stained carpet, and the filth throughout the kitchen. To us it
was a piece of property we believed had the equity in it once we
remodeled it. Other people saw the dirt, we saw the remodeled
house—we saw the end from the beginning.

You may be looking in your checkbook, or at your life, but that's not the place to look. You need to look to the omnipotent One who is all powerful; the omnipresent One who is present in all places at the same time; the omniscient One who is all knowing. That person is Jesus, the author and finisher of your faith (Heb. 12:2), who knows and declares the end from the beginning (Isa. 46:10)—the One who you can believe in to bring everything you desire to pass.

When you look to Jesus, in time you can physically live the life of a winner that you envision on the inside of you. Actually, before you can ever be defeated, He must first get defeated, and that will never happen. That's why you can boldly declare from 1 John 4:17, "As He is, so [am I] in this world," and keep in mind that Jesus is a winner.

One thing the Bible says pertaining to this verse is that we are seated with Him now in heavenly places (Eph. 2:6)—and that's talking about the place of a winner. So while in the natural you may not be a winner at the moment, spiritually speaking, you are not where you physically are as far as God is concerned.

Physically, you may be sitting where you are sitting or standing, feeling like a loser; but spiritually, you are more real up in the "heavenly places" than you are down here, and God sees you as a winner. So you are a winner, whether or not you like it, believe it, or look it right now—because as He is, so are you in this world.

Good Success

The good news is that you can make whatever life you want. It may be more of a challenge for a person who had a bad experience in childhood or while growing up to believe that they can have a good life, but I'm telling you it is not impossible—not if you invite God in to help you. We should never be afraid to ask for help, especially from God. I like to think of it this way: God gave you the gift of life, and whatever you do with it is a gift back to Him, and yet He is near to you to help you give yourself back to Him.

I remember when I was at the end of my rope in life, just barely hanging on. I needed help, so one day I went to this large church building that had a chapel in it. I walked inside, laid on the carpet, and prayed to God. I asked Him to help me and to just tell me what He wanted me to do. I wanted to know what my purpose was for being here on this earth, feeling that if He was God, then He should know.

I stayed there until I got an answer, and when I stood up, I knew in my heart what it was. I had total peace and joy that I had found my purpose in life—and the funny thing was, I was having success in the radio broadcasting world at the time. I was a radio announcer for a top radio station in my area, and people everywhere knew my stage name (I didn't use my real name, the management changed it), but I wasn't happy with my life. I had success (I thought it was) and I had money, but I wasn't happy because I was serving money and had left God out.

Many people associate money with success and they can relate to this; maybe you can too. But when I learned that there was worldly success and then another level of success—which is called *good success* according to God's Word (Joshua 1:8)—I just didn't want success any longer, I wanted this good success. What's the difference?

I wanted to please God and not just me. I truly wanted the void in my life to be filled, and the popularity, the success, and the money I had did not fill the emptiness I felt inside. The reason is that God created every person with a void in their life and designed us in such a way that only He can fill it. Now I have my priorities right—I have God first and everything else that is important to me follows my relationship with Him. I have good success—I have God, my wife and family, and I have peace and happiness.

God also has given me many great people to help fulfill the vision I have for my life, which is from Him. Oh yes, I have money too, but money is just a tool to bring about everything that is necessary for life and for the covenant of God (the Good News) to be established in the lives of people on this earth. People need money, of course, but first of all they need hope and they need God.

Inviting the Greater One—God—into your life is the number one thing you can do to embark on this life as a winner.

When the Greater One lives in you, you are somebody special—you are already a winner, and you can succeed against all odds. Being a winner begins with surrendering your life to Him. Then you can start this exciting lifestyle of winning, yet not just winning but winning against all odds.

Building a Solid Foundation

At the very beginning of time, God gave man and woman everything necessary to win. He spoke to them and told them that they were to be fruitful and multiply. (See Gen. 1:28.) He told them that they had dominion, rule, and power—the right to govern—over everything He had created. (v. 28.) All that was lost because of the disobedience of one couple, Adam and Eve (Gen. 3:1-6), but you probably can understand this.

How many times have you made a wrong decision in life and it cost you a friendship or a relationship or money? You certainly paid the price for your wrong decision. We have all made some foolish mistakes and paid dearly for them. I personally got tired of making the same old mistakes. I was tired of losing out in life and I wanted to be a winner, but I just didn't know where to start.

After finding the starting line when I cried out to God in that chapel, I could enter the race and run to win because the race is not against anyone; it's against the odds that were set before me. It doesn't matter what the odds are that you will encounter (like your ethnic background or your gender); you can overcome them and walk in victory when you build your life on a foundation that is rock-solid. (See Luke 6:48; 1 Cor. 3:11.)

To be a winner you must have a solid foundation to weather the storms of life, something that has been tested and proven to stand against all odds. Then once the storm is over you can still be standing, having won against every adversity.

In the same way a building needs a solid foundation, you need a solid foundation because you are building or rebuilding your life. What will be your foundation—gambling, luck, chance, the world's idea of success? These do not offer anything solid to build on; they are a foundation made of sand. (See Luke 6:49.)

The only firm foundation to build upon is Jesus, who is the rock of our strength (Ps. 92:15), the Word made flesh (John 1:14), the Word of God (Rev. 19:13). I chose Him and the greatest book in the world—the Bible—as my solid foundation, and I have never regretted it. It's a fact that the Bible is the most read book ever. In my opinion it is still the greatest book around that can solve every life issue, and the life principles in it are just astounding.

I have found a new life and winning principles that took me from a lousy life to an exciting one through the Word of God, and I want to share them with you. As I have promised you before, I will tell you only what will work. For this reason, I will be speaking about the Word of God throughout this book. It will be our foundation on which to build a winning life because it gives us the ways to win against all odds.

Notice I said the Word of God. When I use that term, I am talking about the Bible. The Bible is a way that God can talk to every person on this earth. Our life is shaped by words that we have heard and believed over the years; they have made our foundation. If yours has been made with negative words, you can remake your foundation by the words God has spoken to us in the Bible.

Let's start with a verse from the Word that talks about being an overcomer—an important element for a winning life.

*Whatever is born of God **overcomes** the world. And this is the **victory** that has overcome [or overcomes] the world—our faith.*

1 John 5:4

Notice this verse starts with the word *whatever.* The Greek translation for *whatever* also means *whosoever.*[2] So we actually could substitute the word *whosoever* in this verse because it does not matter who you are—if you are a child of God, you can be an overcomer.

Then it says, "This is the victory that has overcome the world." In other words, the apostle John is saying to us that if a person is born of God, that person has become *a born* winner. It is true that

God created man, but this verse is not saying *created by* God, but *born of* God.

I'm sure you have heard of born losers. In everything they do, they feel like it is a loss; they are not making it much in life with anything. You probably know people who believe this about themselves and, in reality, may be living this way. Perhaps you even feel that you are a born loser.

Maybe you grew up in a negative environment, and it formed a losing mentality in you. As a result, your whole life has spoken volumes, saying, *I'm a loser. Everything I do goes wrong, everything I try goes sideways. I can never win.* You may have said this repeatedly to yourself. You really feel like you were just born this way, that it's just the way it is—*a born loser.*

If that's the way you feel, then I say to you, "Get born again and become a born winner." I strongly encourage you to make this first and most important step because this type of person will overcome. This person is not *trying* to overcome, they are *born* to overcome, which means they can prevail over any circumstances in their life. That's being an overcomer.

Isn't this exciting news? It doesn't matter who you are, all you need to do to be qualified to have this working in your life is to be born again. That is the first step. Now, you may be wondering what that term means. Of course I am not talking about going back into your mother's womb. That's impossible. I'm talking about another type of birth that's spiritual in nature.

> *"They are reborn—not with a physical birth resulting from human passion or plan, but a birth that comes from God."*
>
> John 1:13 NLT

Sometimes people are not taught regarding this important truth, they are just told to go to church. But this birth can actually happen in your own home, in your car, any place you can pray, not just in a church. Going to church is important, but the Bible does not say whoever goes to the church overcomes the world. It says *whoever is born of God.*

Right at this point you may be saying to yourself, *But I know some churchgoing people and they are not winners. They are not winning against all odds. They are not overcomers, they are being overcome.* Perhaps this is because they lack knowledge.

New from the Inside Out

My people are destroyed for lack of knowledge.

Hosea 4:6

Maybe you have heard the saying that knowledge is power. There is some truth to that statement, but the best way to look at it is the way God looks at it. He said in this verse that His people are destroyed (or torn down) because of their lack of knowledge. I believe that being torn down is not your vision for your life anymore, or you would not be reading this book. Instead, you want a built-up life, a successful life in all areas.

You are going to find out in these pages how to achieve that. I will be teaching you and giving profound examples of how God's power and ability can work through you to cause you to be a winner. God has the ability to cause those who trust in Him to win against all odds. In the process, the outcome somehow and someway always comes out for the good. Remember, to be a true winner in life begins with being born again. That is the first and most important step to take to win against all odds.

We need God's help to be winners, and I believe you would agree with me that we need His help 24 hours a day, 7 days a week, 365 days a year. It's sad, but the truth is, only in devastating times in our country do we as a nation call on God. We wait until the unthinkable happens, and then we invite the nation to pray. Why not invite God into our lives every day? Why not spend daily time learning about Him and building a relationship with Him? Do you really win in life by shutting God out of it?

What does it profit a man or woman, if he or she gains (wins) the whole world (only material wealth) and loses his or her soul? (See Matt. 16:26.) In other words, if someone seems to be successful but leaves God out of their lives, ultimately that person is still a loser.

Think about this for a moment: Do you know that you and I were a microscopic part of the first man and woman on this earth? You see, all of us were there in the Garden of Eden, and every human being is a descendant of Adam and Eve. To understand this will enlighten your understanding of why it is important for every person to be born again, so what do I mean?

We can look at sin as committing a crime, and we know that there are only negative consequences for any person who does that. It is true for the sin Adam and Eve committed too—and we are still suffering the consequences. When they chose to disobey God by eating the fruit from a tree that was forbidden to them (Gen. 3:6), they put all humankind in the position of death. This death was twofold.

The first death was a spiritual death, which is a separation from God. Adam and Eve enjoyed daily fellowship with God, and this wrongful act stopped that by putting a wedge between them and God. Sin had now taken over their lives, and the life they once knew and lived would be changed forever.

The second death Adam and Eve (and ultimately every other human being) would experience would be physical death. The fact is that every person now living will one day no longer exist in this body because death is inevitable. It may not be a pleasant subject to talk about, but it's the truth.

Adam and Eve really messed it up for us, but Jesus paid the ultimate sacrifice to restore a once broken relationship between God and every human being. Now the only way we can experience the life we should have had with Him—the life of a winner—is to be born again. Once we welcome Jesus into our hearts by saying a simple prayer of invitation and surrender, we immediately are born again—and we become a born winner. Yes, it's that easy and fast. (If you haven't prayed that kind of prayer yet, and would like to, there's a prayer you can pray at the end of this book.)

Can you see now why every person, because of sin, really is a born loser at his or her physical birth? The reason is that they are born into a sin nature. But once you become born again, you do away with being a born loser and you become a born winner.

So winners and losers are both born, not bred. In other words, it doesn't matter what pedigree you come from on this physical planet or what ethnicity or background or neighborhood you grew up in, you have been programmed to ultimately eternally lose. That's why being born again does matter to you.

Maybe you came from a lineage that you are ashamed of. Perhaps you have a family tree that includes losers, drunkards, gamblers, drug addicts, or prostitutes and you want to break free from this cycle. You *can* break free but only by this new birth I have been talking about.

The reason is that you are a spiritual being. You live in a body, and you possess a soul, which includes your mind, will, and emotions; but the real you—the spirit part of you—we cannot see, and your spirit is what's born again. This is called the new birth, because a new spirit will be born in you when you accept Jesus.

Once you are reborn you will have a new outlook on life because you will be new from the inside out. That is the second thing you must do to live as a winner in this life—you must see yourself as God sees Himself. He is a winner, the Greater One who now lives inside of you. Is it any wonder that becoming born again makes you new from the inside out? In a moment, we will see the importance of this, but know that you are a born winner, which qualifies you in God's kingdom as being an overcomer.

What are we trying to overcome? If we are trying to overcome the world, what is it? What are we talking about? Are we trying to climb on this big blue marble called planet Earth and just overcome this big ball? What are we trying to do? Most people don't have a clue, but from this day forward you will know.

It may shock you because most of what you are really trying to overcome is sitting in your house. In fact, if you walked up to a mirror right now, you would see what you are trying to overcome in this world the most…you! In other words, we must work on *us* to win against all odds.

The process of winning starts with working on self. Self must live in this world as long as self has a physical body. That's why the new birth is so important; it not only affects our spirit, but our body and soul as well.

There are basic things we deal with in everyday life that are important to understand—especially our body, soul, and spirit. Everything is not spiritual. Many things are natural—things we must conquer in this world and overcome and not allow to control our lives. So how these three areas can work together or against each other is the critical point for you to learn.

Basically, if they work against each other, you will have chaos; if they work together, you will have won against the odds.

To understand how creatively God made man and woman with the ability to dominate on this earth and control their lives, you need to have a basic knowledge of the body, soul, and spirit of the human race. We are going to cover them next because I believe that this will give you the wisdom you need to know how to best handle your own life and be a winner in everything you do.

CHAPTER 2

The ABC's of the Body, Soul, and Spirit—Part 1

One day when my first granddaughter was about three years old, I was driving down the street and she was in the backseat of the car in her car seat. (My wife and I were babysitting her.) I was using my cell phone, and after I made my call, I turned to her and showed her the cell phone. I asked her if she knew what it was, and she looked strangely at it, so I said to her, "This is a helicopter," and I told her to say *helicopter.*

Later on that day, I asked her again, "What is this?" and this time she answered "helicopter" with no hesitation. Even at three she could articulate words very well. My wife heard us talking and jumped in the conversation, saying, "It is not a helicopter but a cell phone." She didn't understand that I wasn't trying to be mean to my granddaughter; I was trying to prove a point that I had made earlier to my wife about training children correctly at an early age. They are so open to learn as soon as they enter the world.

Did my granddaughter believe that it was really a helicopter? You can answer that for yourself. Just recently, my wife held up her cell phone to display it to our granddaughter, who is now eight (at the time of this writing), and asked her what it was. Our granddaughter responded by saying, "It's a cell phone." And then my wife asked her, "What did Grandpa say this was?" She responded, "A helicopter," and we all laughed. Now she knew the purpose of the cell phone and how to use it.

We can relate that story to ourselves. When you know the purpose and how to effectively use to the best of your ability your body, soul, and spirit, you have gained the proper knowledge that will lead you to a better life. We already saw that we can be destroyed, or be losers, for lack of knowledge, right? As you read this book you are gaining the knowledge you need to change your life for the better.

Human beings were created differently than the angels, including Satan (who is a fallen angel). The Word says that God is a Spirit and we are, in essence, spirit beings, created in His likeness. (See Gen. 1:26.) Yet every human being on the face of this earth also has a body and possesses a soul, which is your mind, will, and emotions. Let's look at an illustration of them from the Bible.

> The word of God is living and active. Sharper than any double-edged sword, it penetrates even to dividing soul and spirit, joints and marrow; it judges the thoughts and attitudes of the heart.
>
> Hebrews 4:12 NIV

Notice this verse says that the Word of God is living (or alive), and active (or operative), energizing, and effective. In other words, when you read the Bible—the words that God has said—you are reading words that are alive, they are living, and when applied to your life, they will effectively work. You can't see the words working, but if you believe and declare them, they will work on your behalf. Notice what else they will do.

The Word of God will divide, or separate, the soul from the immortal spirit, and it will separate the joints and marrow, which represent the body. In his Bible commentary, Matthew Henry explains this separation as the Word cutting "off the lusts of the flesh [physical body] as well as the lusts of the mind."[1] What you do can hinder having a better life.

The writer of Hebrews was talking about the Word dividing the spiritual from the carnal, yet clearly he defined, just in this passage, that the soul, spirit, and body are seen on three different levels.

You cannot treat these three entities as the same. They have different purposes, and to know the use of each one will help you to effectively use all three. It is like having a car. You must know the purpose for a car to use it correctly.

Let's say that a person who lived in the jungle on an unknown island was brought into civilization. Then someone gave this person a car thinking that everyone knows the purpose of a car. Of course a car is to be driven, but this person, on the first day of receiving the car, sits in the car with the one who gave it and says, "How do I fly it?" The other person responds by saying, "What do you mean, how do you fly it? You can't fly it, you must drive it."

Can you see why knowing the purpose of a thing will help you to properly use it? So we're going to look at the ABC's of understanding the body, soul, and spirit because understanding them will take you to another dimension in your life—a life of victory, not a life of being a victim. That is what God desires for you, but you have a choice because you have a will.

God did not create you like a robot. Good or bad, we make choices every day. For the bad choices we have made and will make (not habitually or intentionally), God gives us mercy, and through mercy comes victory. That was the purpose for sending His Son Jesus to the cross, not only for our sins (the messes we made) but because God loves us so much.

God so loved the world that He gave his only begotten Son, that whoever believes in Him should not perish but have everlasting life.

John 3:16

We saw earlier that Christ was a replacement for our sins. That is how God redeemed us back. It's really a love relationship between God and humans. It wasn't just because of the negative sin in our lives; it was because of the positive—"God so loved…"— and He still loves every person on this earth and has everlasting mercy for each of us.

There is nothing we can do to make God hate us. He will judge the sin and hate the deed (the action) of a person, but not the person themselves. By sending His only Son as a sacrifice, we are brought back to the rightful position in Him—the position of victorious living. Are you ready to become a victor instead of a victim?

The Body

The only reason you need a body is so you can live on earth. It is your "earth suit." Your body, or your flesh, was never meant to rule over you. It was given to you by God to help you function while you are alive in this world. When you die you will not need this type of body. According to the Bible, you will receive a new body because your present body will be of no use to you anymore.

This corruptible must put on incorruption, and this mortal must put on immortality. So when this corruptible has put on incorruption, and

this mortal has put on immortality, then shall be brought to pass the
saying that is written: "Death is swallowed up in victory."

1 Corinthians 15:53,54

When we are out of this body, we are immediately with the Lord. Death is not the end of life, because our soul and spirit will exit the body and will live on forever, either in heaven or in hell. For Christians, that place will be in heaven with the Lord for all eternity.

We are confident, yes, well pleased rather to be absent from the body
and to be present with the Lord.

2 Corinthians 5:8

This is one of the reasons why we should not worship our body. The body is important, but it has its proper place. It is important to stay focused on worshipping the Creator and not the creation. We are to worship God and Him alone. Thank God for the trees, the earth, the stars, the animals, and all humans—with God in your life you will know how to properly treat everything that He created—but none of them is to be worshipped. In fact, your body is to be used only to glorify God. (See 1 Cor. 6:20.)

Your physical senses function through the body. I'm sure you know that the five senses are sight, taste, touch, hearing, and smell. Of course, you use your eyes to see, your mouth to taste, your hands to touch, your ears to hear, and your nose to smell. We truly are an incredible working machine, specially designed by God. Without these important functions, we would be limited to the intake of the material world around us—and if we are limited with what we can physically take in by any one of our five senses, we can be limited in what we can put out.

I have heard of some wonderful people who did not allow their limitations to hinder their progress. I recall one particular story about a young lady who was paralyzed after a skiing accident in which she lost her mobility from the neck down. The use of her hands and her legs was gone, but the use of her brain was still intact.

She was gifted in the area of painting, but because of the limitation of using her hands, she could not hold the paintbrush in her hands. Instead, she would hold the paintbrush between her lips—and paint beautiful pictures. Not being able to use her hands did not stop her from painting; she just found another way to paint.

If the desire in you is God-given, then there will be a natural God-driven attitude to get it done.

As you can tell, your body is needed to carry out natural functions in a natural world. Every part of your physical body is considered a member, so if you use your body to fulfill unrighteousness, then you will reap corruption. This is important to know because I have been talking about winning against *all* odds, and there is a negative cause and effect for using your body in an unrighteous lifestyle.

Look at this negative scenario, "You have sown much, and bring in little; you eat, but do not have enough; you drink, but you are not filled with drink; you clothe yourselves, but no one is warm; and he who earns wages, earns wages to put into a bag with holes." Thus says the Lord of hosts: "Consider your ways!" (Haggai 1:6-7). Notice that there was no satisfaction, no matter what was being done; there was no positive outcome. Wouldn't this be a lousy way to live? You try this and you try that, but nothing works.

That's why we must consider our ways. What are we doing? What lifestyle choices are being made that are hindering success? Take inventory in the area of your flesh, your physical body. What are you doing with what belongs to God?

The Bible tells us that we are bought at a price (1 Cor. 7:23)— Jesus paid the price with His life on the cross. Therefore, we are to honor God with our body. The truth is, once you become born again, you are not your own.

You may say to yourself, *I don't believe all this,* but it really doesn't matter because it doesn't change the fact that Jesus died for your sins. It doesn't change what happened. He still died and He still rose from the grave and He still is alive, sitting at the right hand of God in heaven. Jesus did all this to carry out God's plan for mankind to be redeemed from the wages of death. So with your body you are to honor God.

Some people do honor God with their body and some people don't, but it still doesn't change the purpose for it. God left this choice up to us individually, and we will reap the consequences, good or bad, according to what we choose. God wants us to choose the good way; it's an open-book test.

> *This day I call heaven and earth as witnesses against you that I have set before you life and death, blessings and curses. Now **choose life**, so that you and your children may live.*
>
> Deuteronomy 30:19 NIV

This is the only way to truly live a life filled with purpose. When we choose life, we are choosing God's way of doing and being right. There are some practical life choices that must be made to experience an abundant life. It's just like baking a cake— you must have the right ingredients to get the picture-box results—and the best place to find the right ingredients to get a successful life is in the Bible.

For example, from the verse above we see that when we allow the flesh to rule, it will be detrimental to us and our children. The negative choices we make as adults can affect even our children. But, taking control over your flesh is life. It's a blessing to be in control of your own body. You tell your flesh what it will and will not do. It is truly liberating to no longer be in bondage under the mere elements of the flesh.

This is only one area of choosing life, but it is the most needed area to look at because so many people are defeated not by the devil, but by their own flesh. Here's a Scripture passage on what we've been talking about that I believe will be helpful to you.

> *Therefore do not let sin reign in your mortal body, that you should obey it in its lusts. And do not present your members as instruments of unrighteousness to sin, but present yourselves to God as being alive from the dead, and your members as instruments of righteousness to God.... What fruit did you have then in the things of which you are now ashamed?... For the wages of sin is death [or separation from God], but the gift of God is eternal life in Christ Jesus our Lord.*
>
> Romans 6:12-13,21,23

As you know, *members* refers to your body. You can use your members as weapons to do wrong or as a way to present yourself to God and glorify Him. Can you see how valuable your body is? Can you see that every day you live on earth, you have a choice to use your body for good works or for bad works?

You are a steward of what belongs to God. If people really think they own themselves, then why don't they stop themselves from dying and from leaving their body here? We brought nothing into this world and we can carry nothing from it.

Allow me to get "real" here. At any funerals you've attended have you ever seen a casket filled with cars or houses or money or other material possessions? Probably not; I know I haven't. But I have seen, and I'm sure you have too, a body lying there in a casket with no movement whatsoever. There is no longer life in that body, and whatever visions were left undone through that body are no longer capable of being completed.

It's a sad thought that in the graveyard are many buried dreams. That's why I will be talking about your dreams and visions in this book. I am determined to use my body until it wears out, fulfilling every possibility that is set before me. And I'm determined to convince every person with whom I come in contact to fulfill their dreams, even if man thinks they're impossible, because each person can, with God's help—for all things are possible with God. (Mark 9:23.) How about you?

The Soul

These three components make up your soul—your mind, your will, and your emotions. We are going to go over all three so that you can understand their importance and how to use each of them to your advantage. Your mind, will, and emotions can work for you or against you, so you need to learn how to get them to work for you. Let's begin with the mind.

The Mind.

Your mind is basically the seat of your intellect (your ability to reason or understand), and your thoughts (the act or process of thinking). Thoughts become habits and habits become your lifestyle, or the way you live. The way you think is primarily developed by what you put into your mind—the books you read, the people you associate with, the television (or "tell-a-vision") programs you watch, the radio stations you listen to faithfully, what you look at on the Internet, the type of preaching you hear on a regular basis, the occupation you are involved with.

I remember when I decided to learn to fly an airplane. The first thing I did was go to my local bookstore and buy a book on the subject. As I read the book, my interest was ignited in this area and today I have many pilot ratings of various types of aircrafts, including a helicopter. That was the result of reading one book and attaining many flight hours after years of schooling. I'm telling you all this because my mind had to adjust to a new way of thinking regarding flight.

It's a whole different ball game than driving a car. For one thing, I had to think and talk like a pilot. So I started to listen to air traffic control on a regular basis. I cannot tell you the countless number of books and flight magazines I have read, and still read, to keep me informed of the currents trends and other technical information that will be helpful for my safety and those who fly with me. All this is for the purpose of programming my thoughts in this particular area.

I have other areas of interest that are not related to flight, and I read related materials to get my mind thinking the kind of thoughts needed to master those areas. You have probably heard the adage "You are what you eat," but I say "You are what you think," for as a person thinks in their heart so are they. (See Prov. 23:7) If you think you are a winner, you will be one. If you think you are a loser, you will be a loser. What do you set your mind on?

It's best to set your mind on thoughts that will cause you to win. When you set your mind on something day and night, you are actually taking another step, which is called *meditation*. I'm not talking about what some false religions teach their followers. Day and night your mind should be filled with only thoughts that will lead you into a victorious life.

This will take discipline because our carnal mind will try to take over, but I submit to you that the Bible is the best book for you to get your mind fixed on. In the Bible is everything you need to get your mind thinking the right way, which will give you the end results you desire.

> *This Book of the Law shall not depart out of your mouth, but you shall meditate on it day and night, that you may observe and do according to all that is written in it. For then you shall make your way prosperous, and then you shall deal wisely and have good success.*
>
> Joshua 1:8 AMP

Who is responsible for you having good success? It's not your professor or the preacher—it's *you!* These kinds of people are in your life to help you and they are responsible to feed you knowledge, but ultimately it is you who will be held accountable for what you do with the knowledge you gain through them.

God is not responsible for your lack of success or having good success either. He tells us to take His Word (the Book of the Law) and meditate on it consistently. The word *meditate* is very interesting. It means to "ponder."[2] When you ponder you are thinking deeply or in deep thought about something, and we are told to ponder on the Word of God, or think deeply about what it is saying to us personally. How does that particular word or verse relate to your situation?

The word *ponder* means to "consider."[3] What will you decide to do after mediating on or considering a particular word or Scripture? Allow me to give you an example.

Let's say that you have a desire to better your marriage. We all know that it takes effort to make a marriage work, but did you know that the Bible is the best textbook on the matter? In fact, I believe the Bible is the best textbook regarding any subject. That is why I give many Scriptures throughout this book. As I said at the beginning, I believe the Bible is a solid foundation, and if you are building a great life—having a desire to do above average things, not living a mediocre life—then I recommend it.

A professional builder will tell you that the higher the building you want to build, the deeper the foundation must be. So the higher you want to go in life, the deeper your relationship to God and His Word should become. It's the Word of God speaking to our hearts in a practical, down-to-earth way that's going to help us to win.

So, you want to better your marriage, and while reading the Bible one day you run across this Scripture, "Husbands, love your wives [be affectionate and sympathetic with them] and do not be harsh or bitter or resentful toward them" (Col. 3:19 AMP). First you stop and you mediate on what you just read; then you must decide what you will do with it or if you are going to do *anything* with it.

If you decide to use it, then you have made a decision to work on your marriage, because now you have something to shape the way you think toward your wife. It is telling you to treat her with affection and sympathy, or you could use the word *consideration*.

Now you know what to do, and you say to yourself, *I will become more loving, and a more considerate husband. My wife may upset me sometimes, but I will not resent her. I will show her my love expressed in words and deeds.* What have you just done? You have added a success principle to your life, and as you continue to choose to obey this word, you will enjoy good success in your marriage.

The same holds true for a wife. You can find Scriptures in the Bible that will tell you how to treat your husband.

Another meaning for the word *meditation* is the word *imagine.* We will discuss this more later on, but you will make your own way successful by having a mental image of what you desire. This is godly.

If you know the story about Abraham, he was very old, way past the age of having children, and his wife was advanced in age as well. She too was past the age of bearing children—but God gave Abraham a promise, which included a child. To show Abraham how many descendants he would have, God took Abraham outside and told him to look up toward heaven and count the stars. (See Gen. 15:5.) When Abraham looked up, he started to count, but no way was it possible to do, for there were too many.

Do you know what God was doing? He was giving Abraham a mental picture of the promise He had made to him.

I can imagine Abraham getting ready for bed and closing his eyes and imagining the stars and what they represented to him. That mental picture stayed fixed in his mind as long as he was alive, and through some of the odds that were against him, he kept focused on the mental image God gave to him.

As much as possible, I keep visual and mental pictures in my mind for what I desire to come to pass in my life. I have often put pictures on my refrigerator of various things I desired and have seen each one come to pass. In my mind I saw myself flying a plane before I actually flew a plane. I went through many processes in my imagination—how to start the plane, how to taxi the plane, how to land the plane—before I actually got in a plane and successfully accomplished every task.

Perhaps you want to be a good husband or a good wife, or maybe you have a desire to become something else—a business owner, a pastor, or a nurse, for example. *See* yourself as one. Fix in your mind what you want to do and just do it. You can become what you think.

The Will.

The second area of the soul is the *will*. The best way to explain this is the example that Jesus left us.

Prior to Jesus' death on the cross, He spent some time just praying in the Garden of Gethsemane. He was in much anguish, and after kneeling down to pray, He addressed His Father and said, "O My Father, if it is possible, let this cup pass from Me; nevertheless, not as I will, but as You will" (Matt. 26:39). It was possible for God to intervene, and for this reason Jesus had to get His own will involved in the divine plan of God.

When Jesus made the choice to do God's will, that sealed it, and now we are the fruit of that hard decision Jesus made in the garden without the support of His own disciples, for they were asleep. When we say yes to God's will for our lives, we say yes to success. God's will is His Word and He is our Creator, but He cannot change our will, neither will He try to control it.

Some athletes are free to sign a contract with any team and they are called free agents. We too are free agents, in a sense.

Anytime we want, we can do our own thing. Bad choices will lead to bad consequences, and good choices will lead to good consequences, but the choice is final with us. When we "will" to do the right thing with the right purpose, we can have, in due time, at the appointed season, victory.

I encourage you to set your will at a higher level by the Word of God, and without any unnecessary delays, so you can reap a harvest of blessings.

Our Emotions.

Our emotions can be unstable and not reassuring at times (I believe my wife would say a big *amen* to this), but we all have them and we must know how to handle them because if they get the best of us, they can cause much devastation. Yet, our emotions could very well be the needed feelings that compel us to make positive choices. So putting aside all of the psychological emotional disorders like depression, suicidal thoughts, emotional abuse, and anxiety, I want to shed some light regarding this complex area in a simple way.

First let me say that if you do believe that you have any emotional disturbances, I strongly encourage you to seek professional help, including talking to the spiritual leader in your life, like your pastor. The Bible says, "In the multitude of counsellors [the right counselors] there is safety" (Prov. 11:14 KJV). Never feel ashamed in reaching out for help because then people can reach in to help you.

Now, let's move on to the various types of emotions that are sometimes manifested outwardly.

Anger: Anger is not a sin. If it was, then Jesus sinned. And if that were true, then He was not perfect. From the Bible we know that Jesus was tempted, but yet He never sinned. Let's look at the anger that was expressed by Him in two different situations.

On one particular Sabbath day, a man with a withered hand was sitting in the synagogue when Jesus entered there. No doubt this man wanted Jesus to make his hand whole again. But as Jesus' critics watched to see if He would heal this man on a Sabbath, the Bible says that Jesus looked around at them with anger, then spoke to the man with the withered hand and told him to stretch out his hand. (See Mark 3:5.) When the man obeyed the words spoken to him, his hand was made whole.

Notice that Jesus looked at them with anger, yet He wasn't aggressive. I'm sure you would agree that Jesus was a meek person, but meekness is not weakness. Meekness is strength under control.

Another case in point was the time that Jesus went to Jerusalem for the annual Jewish Passover celebration. When He arrived, He saw merchants selling various wares in the temple. Jesus made a whip from small cords and chased these people out of there and turned over tables where the moneychangers were doing business. (John 2:13-16.) What was this display of emotion by Jesus? It was a very intense emotion called *passion.*

What are you passionate about? Jesus was very passionate about His Father's house. This wasn't physical abuse, because Jesus just chased them out brandishing a whip; He didn't actually strike anyone with it. But I want you to see that this emotion can cause you to stand up and be counted when righteousness is being jeopardized. That day His disciples recalled what was written by David hundreds of years earlier, "Zeal for your house will consume me" (John 2:17 NIV).

On the other hand, the anger of Cain led him to murder his own brother. (See Gen. 4:8.) What is the difference between the anger that Jesus had and Cain's anger? This is very important because you will experience anger, and what you do with it will determine if your outcome will be successful or not.

In the course of time, Cain took an offering to God, but his motive and his offering weren't the best he could give. His brother, Abel, took an offering as well, but his motive and his offering were his best because God accepted what Abel took but not what Cain took. (See Gen. 4:3-5.) So Cain was exceedingly angry and the Bible says that his countenance fell, which means that he looked sad and depressed. (See v. 6.)

His emotions changed, and when they did, his face took on another appearance. Proverbs 15:13 NIV says, "A happy heart makes the face cheerful," but in Cain's situation he allowed his anger to get the best of him. When God saw it, he tried to warn Cain that if he didn't master his emotions, he would do something wrong. (See Gen. 4:6-7 NIV.) We too have the ability to change how we feel.

If God told Cain he could master his emotions and put anger aside, then we have the ability to do the same as well. Yet Cain didn't listen to correction; he yielded to his emotions and committed murder. But Jesus just moved on to the next thing on His agenda. He was angry only for a moment—and that is about how long anyone has a right to be angry.

When God gets angry, the Bible says that it lasts only a moment. (See Ps. 30:5.) One of the Hebrew words for *moment* is "raga" (raw gah'), which means a wink.[4] Another word is "rega" (reh' gah), meaning a very short space of time.[5] Blink your eyes and that's it. So it's best to take control of this emotion quickly: "He that is soon angry [quick tempered] dealeth foolishly" (Prov. 14:17 KJV); "Don't make friends with people who have hot, violent tempers. You might learn their habits and not be able to change" (Prov. 22:24–25 TEV).

It's wise not to hang out or associate with people who are always angry about everything imaginable. Bad company can corrupt good manners. To help you, here are ten winning ways to overcome anger.

1. Blink your eyes. You have only a moment.

2. Turn your focus to a project. Get your mind off the problem.

3. Get a cheerful face. Go do something that will bring you joy. Get away from the situation.

4. Go talk to a trusted friend who will help you to calm down, not stir up more strife.

5. Seek spiritual guidance.

6. Read a favorite passage in the Bible (I suggest Psalm 23) and meditate on it.

7. Think on the things that are true, honorable, pure, lovely, and of a good report. Think good thoughts.

8. Go cheer someone else up. "He who refreshes others will himself be refreshed" (Prov. 11:25 NIV).

9. Get professional help if needed.

10. Pray to God for His help.

Worry is another emotion that is similar to anger in that it must be mastered in order for you to win against all odds. Do you know that you can stop worrying? Worrying sometimes is a habit or it is generated from fear. It could be fear of failure, fear of the unknown, fear of dying, fear of not having enough.

Worry comes through some type of door that is left open in your heart, but you can put a stop to worry and get on the road to a worry free life. I am not saying that you will not be challenged to worry again, we all are. But you can refuse to worry, and let it pass by. Here are some practical steps you can take to assist you in putting a stop to worry in this process of becoming worry free.

1. Write down your concerns and present them to God. Say a simple prayer asking God to help you regarding every area that you have written down. Then throw the paper away as an act of believing that God heard you and now He is helping you. Expect to get wisdom and direction as you continue your daily work.

2. Fix your mind on what is positive.

3. Devote yourself to the teachings of Jesus.

4. Refuse to live an idle life. Learn something new, maybe something you have put off for years that you always wanted to do. At 48 years old, I started flight school. You are never too young or too old to learn something new.

5. Get active in your church and meet new friends.

6. Eat healthy and exercise regularly. Exercising releases endorphins, a natural pain reliever.

You can become worry free by taking these steps of faith toward your freedom from worries and giving them to God. When you know that God is working in you, your soul will prosper, which is a step toward your success.

A By-product of Prosperity

Soul prosperity is not only for you, but for the people around you. Jesus is our greatest example of this truth.

Looking at the Scriptures in John 4, we see Jesus talking to a woman of Samaria, asking her for a drink of water.

This woman went to draw water at the well where Jesus was resting, and He said to her, "'Give Me a drink.' For His disciples had gone away into the city to buy food. Then the woman of Samaria said to Him, 'How is it that You, being a Jew, ask a drink from me, a Samaritan woman?'" (vv. 7-9.)

The Samaritans, being a mixed race, had no dealings with the Jews, and vice versa, yet here was Jesus (a Jew), talking to her, and He answered her question, in essence saying "You don't know who you are talking to." (See v. 10.) Then He told her she had had five husbands and was presently living in adultery.

God was working in the Samaritan woman, and after this conversation, she realized who she was dealing with, saw herself differently—and her soul prosperity rocketed sky high! She ended up taking Jesus' information and telling it to the people in her city. The result was that many of the Samaritans of that city believed because of what she said.

God wants you to be a winner. He wants you to exponentially increase, but His desire for you is that your soul prospers first.

Beloved, I pray that you may prosper in all things and be in health, just as your soul prospers.

3 John 2

When your soul (your mind, will, and emotions) is prospering, then prosperity in all areas on the outside will be a by-product.

CHAPTER 3

The ABCs of the Body, Soul, and Spirit—Part 2

God made us fearfully and wonderfully. (See Ps. 139:14 KJV.) It is amazing to think about how He made us so complex. We have everything we need to do what He said—to be fruitful, to multiply, to subdue and have dominion over the earth and every living thing that moves on the earth. (See Gen. 1:26,28.) God put inside each of us the "right stuff."

We are creatures who can feel things, we can speak, we can think and imagine. That's how many business inventions, plans, and ideas come to pass. God said in Proverbs 8:12 that He gives us witty inventions—He can give us the wisdom and imagination to be able to create what man needs, but not only to make money. He wants us to be able to better ourselves, to better humankind, and to better the kingdom of God. We have our mind, will, emotions, imaginations, and our intellect (and we're thinking all the time) to do that.

In the previous chapter, we looked at these parts of the soulish realm and learned that you are actually a spirit who lives in a physical body that has a soul. The only reason you need a body is because you are on the earth—this earth is the physical residence for every human being, and God gave us a physical body to contain the human spirit.

You are actually a three-part being. God created you in His image; He is a Spirit. (See John 4:24.) So the "real" you is not what you can see on the outside (your physical body), as you are a spirit person. This is how God "put you together—spirit, soul, and body" (1 Thess. 5:23 MSG).

The Greek word for *spirit* is "pneuma," which means "the vital principal by which the body is animated…the power by which the human being feels, thinks, decides."[1] It refers to the higher part or nature of humans[2] and is also defined as "the immaterial and immortal part" of us.[3]

In the Bible, there was a transfiguration where two of the old patriarchs from years gone by, Moses and Elijah, met with Jesus on a certain mountain even though these two distinguished Old Testament people had been dead physically for hundreds of years. This may sound far-fetched, yet three disciples witnessed this meeting—Peter, James, and John—and it was recorded in the New Testament. (See Matt. 17:1-3.)

These transfigured men who went to talk with Jesus were still the same type of people they had been when alive on earth, but they didn't have the same type of physical body. They were still alive spiritually, though their bodies had died years before—proof that when you die, you are not gone. Your spirit will live on forever (either in heaven or hell) because the spirit is immortal and consequently is unaffected by death.[4]

When your physical body dies, you are gone from this planet where we can't handle you, talk to you, hug you, see you, or spend any time with you; but you are still alive in the spiritual realm.

Your soul and your spirit are still operating—you can still think, you can still sense things, and you can still talk, as we just saw.

God's original plan for us revolved around our spirit—to live in a physical body that we control with our spirit—but a lot of us run our lives by our soulish part. For example, your body is not supposed to go down the street to a bar or a club (let alone with somebody you are not married to, if you have a spouse) and get so stone-cold intoxicated that you don't know anything about it the next day. Where was your body yesterday? You should know! You may say, "I don't know, it just went by itself." No, your will (part of your soul) was in control of it.

What are you allowing to be the motivation in your life to control your will?

When you decided to read this book, for example, your will might have said to read this book. Your mind might have objected and said, *Let's go watch TV,* but your will insisted, *We are going to read this book.* Your body may have said, *I don't feel like it; I'd rather go to sleep,* but this time your will yielded to your spirit and said, *We really need what is in this book;* then your spirit agreed, *Yes, we are going to read about the principles of God in this book,* and here you are reading it.

This kind of interaction between your spirit, soul, and body actually goes on 24 hours a day, 7 days a week, but here's something to remember: Your spirit will always go for the spiritual things of God because the spiritual things of God are really what you crave in your spirit.

Thank God, the spirit won with your will in your decision to read this book, but too often the opposite happens in people's lives. That's why it is so important to know how to get your spirit in control of the rest of you.

There are some people who can say, "I don't know why I always get into sexual sins." The reason is that they *want* to go and get into sexual sins; they won't stop themselves. They've allowed their lives to be controlled by their mind and their will instead of their spirit. It's really very simple—they are not attached spiritually to God.

Proverbs 20:27 KJV says, "The spirit of man is the candle of the Lord, searching all the inward parts of the belly." Let's pick this apart for a moment. This term "the spirit of man" is another proof that means you have your own spirit, but here's something else about it. Individuals can influence your human spirit and get you to do the wrong thing or influence you to go the wrong way—the way of a loser—and you'll even wonder how it happened. The reason it happened is that you did not have your spirit controlled by the Holy Spirit.

Perhaps you have recognized yourself in some of this teaching so far and are wondering what you can do about it. People may make decisions with their own will, but those decisions can be affected by their spirit.

When a person is born again, their spirit is reattached to God by His Holy Spirit. That means you are no longer a free moral agent by yourself without any influence from God any longer. You are now back in the relationship that God originally had with Adam in the Garden of Eden before sin came on the scene. You are now reattached spiritually to God.

From that moment on, you have the ability, by the Holy Spirit, to be able to be connected to God and receive into your spirit, by His Spirit, the perfect will of God

> *When He, the Spirit of Truth...comes, He will guide you into all the Truth.... For He will not speak His own message...but He will tell whatever He hears [from the Father;...and He will announce and declare to you the things that are to come [that will happen in the future].*
>
> John 16:13 AMP

You see, the higher part of you, your spirit, is "receptive of the Spirit of God," allying you to Him.[5]

Something else you can do to be controlled by your spirit and not your soul is to pray in the Spirit. We'll discuss this later on, but basically it's praying in a heavenly language given to you by God, which builds up your spirit "on your most holy faith" (Jude 1:20). The reason is the fact that you now are a being who has been connected back to the original Source of who you came from—God, who is a Spirit. His Spirit is "the author and [inditer] of prayer and an assister in it,"[6] and where the Spirit of the Lord is, you are free.

Prophecy of a Winner

Jesus is the perfect example of someone whose life was controlled by His spirit, not His flesh. His life on earth is proof that we can live that way too. In Isaiah 61 the Bible gives a prophecy of what was going to happen to Jesus during His life and that is directly related to what we've been talking about. After we look at this passage, we're going to discuss Luke 4, which is the fulfillment of this prophecy.

Verse 1.

> *"The spirit of the Lord God is upon Me, because the Lord has anointed Me to preach good tidings to the poor; He has sent me to heal the brokenhearted."*

Isaiah 61:1

The first thing we see in this verse that is going to happen with Jesus is, *brokenhearted folks are going to get fixed-up hearts.* Brokenheartedness is rampant in the world today. For instance, many marriage relationships are destroyed and the children are hurt by it too. Some of them even grow up having no idea who their parents are.

Divorces are at an all-time high, and there are so many fatherless homes. Some men suddenly abandon their families and run off to do what they want to do, leaving the women to raise their children by themselves. Then there are those men who find out their wives have been committing adultery.

Whatever the situation may be, whether a marriage problem or something else, brokenhearted people need help and healing.

I'm not against getting godly counseling if it's Bible-based, but psychologists often have the same problems and can't really deal effectively with the issues. They can't totally help people because it takes the Spirit of the living God and His anointing[7] to get to the core of the problems.

Perhaps you are a brokenhearted person. Maybe you've had your heart broken at some point, and you are wearing the spirit of a brokenhearted person—always down and out and upset and hurting all the time. People bring up certain subjects and you don't even want to talk about them because you went through that tough time. You need to know that the anointing of God is available for you; the Spirit of God can empower you and heal your broken heart.

You may have tried to medicate yourself with pills, drugs, alcohol, or all different kinds of relationships to help to cover up that brokenheartedness, but all of that doesn't work. You need the Spirit of the living God to come in and heal that brokenheartedness in you. Are you with me?

"To proclaim liberty [there it is!] to the captives."

Isaiah 61:1

This is also part of verse 1 and talks about freedom in Christ, a powerful statement as people are captive in all kinds of ways. One example I want to use is pornography because of its grip on the minds of so many men and women who are caught up in it. They may be drawn to pornographic magazines, movies, cable TV channels, or certain Web sites regularly, but they all have the same thing in common—they can't stop.

People who are dealing with these things are in bondage. Perhaps you have dealt with this situation and you have been trying to get free. God wants you to know that you can be free. You don't have to be captive to this anymore.

Maybe it's not pornography; maybe it's an addiction to some prescription drug that you have been dealing with, or maybe you are an alcoholic. You need to know that God can set you free. You can win even against sin. You may be captive, but you can be set free. You can't take a pill to get rid of the pills. Freedom comes from the anointing of the Holy Spirit within your life.

For the ones who are captive there is liberty; there is freedom, there is "the opening of the prison to those who are bound" (v. 1). If you have been bound to anything, God wants to set you free.

Verse 2.

"To proclaim the acceptable year of the Lord."

Isaiah 61:2

This verse refers to the Year of Jubilee, which happened every 50 years in Israel, starting with the blowing of the shofar. The Year of Jubilee was a proclamation of liberty representing the release of debts, restoration of inheritances, and cessation of servitude for those who became servants to pay off their debts.[8]

So, for example, if you had lost a house during those 50 years (maybe you didn't handle your finances right), you could go back in the Year of Jubilee and say to whoever took your house, "It is over (like a Monopoly game); give me my house back," and they would have to return it to you. Or maybe you lost your chariot (your car), the same would be true for that. The point is, all you had taken away from you had to be given back to you in that 50th year, after the shofar was blown. Whatever you messed up in and lost, you got it all back.

The blowing of the shofar actually symbolized the voice of Jesus when He would come to proclaim Jubilee in Luke 4. This is what the prophet Isaiah was preaching in Isaiah 61. He was telling us that it is coming to pass when there will be One who comes who will be anointed of God to even proclaim the year of the shofar or the Jubilee forever.

Albert Barnes talks about this in his Bible commentary: "In like manner [of the blowing of the shofar in the year of Jubilee] the

Messiah would come to proclaim universal liberty—liberty to all the world from the degrading servitude of sin. The time of His coming would be a time when [God] would be pleased to proclaim through Him universal emancipation from this ignoble bondage, and to restore to all the privilege of being the freedmen of the Lord."[9]

When you are born again, it's the Year of Jubilee every year for you. You don't have to wait 50 years under Jesus Christ; Jesus became the Jubilee for us so we can be free from poverty, sickness, and sin. It means that it's time to get our "stuff" back.

Years ago I was out in disobedience and didn't know the facets of God that I am sharing with you in this book. I was away from Him, and my wife and I lost a big beautiful house because of it. At the age of 21 we had built a house on acreage overlooking the valley and it had a good view of Mt. Rainier, but we lived in that house only for a short period of time. Certain things that had happened in my life that weren't right opened the door to the enemy and allowed him to take that house from us. We couldn't win for losing due to my disobedient ways.

I'm telling you, nobody could help us win, not even our attorneys, and we lost the house and all that equity—but God knows how to give Jubilee to His children.

Seven blocks from that house is another house, bigger and better. As I began to seek God and learn more about Him, He put in my heart one day while I was praying that this house would be ours.

When we lost the house we had built, we decided to go look for another one. Many years later, after we were restored financially, my wife, children, and I went from one house to another until we walked into one particular house and I said, "This is the house." It was a beautiful house and as soon as we walked through the door I saw that the carpenters were finishing up the kitchen cabinets—the same cabinets that I had seen in my spirit by revelation of the Holy Spirit when I had been praying.

All those wonderful cabinets were also part of the vision and dream that God had given us for our church—that the cabinets in our lives were completely filled and people were coming from all nations and eating of the good gospel food that we had in those cabinets. So, when God showed me the cabinets of this house, it went along with the vision that He had given us in our spirit for our ministry.

The builder didn't really want to sell the house. He was building the house for his girlfriend and was planning to live in the house with her. So he had put thousands of dollars' worth of custom upgrades in it that you wouldn't normally put in a house—but all of a sudden she didn't like the house anymore and didn't want to live there.

I'm here to tell you that seven blocks from where the devil stole from us, God gave us a Jubilee—but He didn't stop there. Over the next few years He blessed us with house after house after house—we acquired so much real estate I forgot which ones were mine." That is winning against all odds!

The Year of Jubilee is here for you too. It's the spirit God wants to put on you.

That same anointing was upon us when we bought our ministry property. We personally wanted to put out the earnest money to buy the property, but God brought thousands of dollars to us for the land, then millions of dollars to build.

I'm talking about the Year of Jubilee; I'm talking about the anointing that we have been walking under. Millions of dollars later that anointing is still working because Jubilee is always right now for born-again believers.

I started realizing that if I lost something (like the house we had built), I needed it back, and soon I found a Scripture in the book of Proverbs that said if the devil stole it, you get it back seven times. (See Prov. 6:31.) Then I understood why we got house after house after house, and commercial property too. God gave us our ministry property and other property around us because every year is the Year of Jubilee for believers and whatever is taken from us, we have a Bible right to get back.

Isaiah 61:2 also mentions "the day of vengeance to our God." That's talking about the Lord's vengeance on Satan, which means that some of your success is payback to the enemy.

Verses 3-4.

> "To appoint unto them that mourn in Zion, to give unto them beauty for ashes, the oil of joy [that's the Holy Spirit] for mourning, the garment of praise for the spirit of heaviness; that they might be called trees of righteousness, the planting of the Lord, that he might be glorified."
>
> Isaiah 61:3 KJV

We can see from this verse that God gives you something for something—like beauty for ashes, oil of joy for mourning, the garment of praise for the spirit of heaviness. The next verse tells you His reason for doing that (I want you to get this):

"They shall build the old wastes, they shall raise up the former deso-
lations, and they shall repair the waste cities, the desolations of
many generations."

Isaiah 61:4 KJV

The point is, you are not blessed just to have something for yourself—you are blessed to be a blessing. You are blessed to be able to help build up things that are torn down and people who are torn down. God wants to bless you so you can help your city. God wants to bless you so you can help children (especially in your area) who are hurting right now. God wants to bless you so you can be a blessing to other people, so that when you hear of somebody in need, you can help them.

We are blessed to help build up broken-down people and places. We are not to win just for ourselves—we are winners to show others how to win.

Verses 5-7.

"Strangers shall stand and feed your flocks, and the son of the alien
shall be your plowman and your vinedressers. But ye shall be named
the Priests of the Lord: men shall call you the ministers of our God;
ye shall eat the riches of the Gentiles, and in their glory shall ye boast.
For your shame ye shall have double; and for confusion they shall
rejoice in their portion: therefore in their land they shall possess the
double, everlasting joy shall be unto them."

Isaiah 61:5-7 KJV

According to this passage, our blessings will "be greatly increased and multiplied,"[10] and we will not be captives anymore—and that's good news!

Let's continue to focus on the spirit of man by looking at the fulfillment of this prophecy.

New Substance of Choice

In Luke 4:17 Jesus came on the scene to fulfill what we just read in Isaiah 61. He made sure that people knew He was confirming this word and it was coming to pass right at that moment. Here's how He did it.

Jesus had been led into the wilderness by the Holy Spirit and had fasted 40 days and 40 nights; then He was tempted by the enemy, Satan, and was victorious over him. The truth is that after Jesus fasted, He was so anointed by the Holy Spirit there was nothing that could defeat Him.

The Matthew 4 version of this story says that after Satan left Jesus, the angels went to minister to Him and He got refreshed. When He returned from that wilderness experience, He went into the synagogue in Nazareth and stood up to read. He grabbed ahold of the scroll of Isaiah that was handed to him, and in the sight of everybody there, He turned to Isaiah 61 and began to preach His first sermon after being anointed and receiving the Spirit of God upon Him. (See Luke 4:16–18.)

I believe that God had Jesus fast for those 40 days and 40 nights so that Jesus would be able to deliver and fulfill this word in Isaiah 61. Let's look at His first message after overcoming the devil's temptation in the wilderness.

> *There was delivered unto him the book of the prophet [Isaiah]. And when he had opened the book, he found the place where it is written, the Spirit of the Lord is upon me, because he hath anointed me to preach the gospel to the poor.*
>
> Luke 4:17-18 KJV

Notice the word *preach* and the first thing Jesus preached on— good news to poor folk. Don't tell me He wants you broke. The first message He preached after He was so anointed was that your finances can change just by the words He spoke. Getting rich should begin with getting preached rich; you have to be preached into prosperity.

I like John Gill's Bible commentary on this. He says that not only are the poor Jesus talked about "sensible of their spiritual poverty" and "seek to Christ for durable riches," but they "frankly acknowledge that all they have and are, is owing to the grace of God."[11]

It's not all about money, of course; "poor" can refer to other areas of our lives too (health, relationships, our souls, for example), but it was the first message Jesus delivered, and money was an important part of it.

Now, I'm not trying to condemn you if you are putting in more than 40 hours on your job every week to get more dollars than anything else; but too often that kind of lifestyle affects others as well as you. For instance, some people don't put that many hours into taking care of their children. They leave those little darlings at a day care, pay them to keep those precious ones until they finish work, and even are willing to pay overtime if they have to do more work to make a few more dollars.

By the time they split off how much the day care costs them, how much frustration it was to get through that traffic and to get back there (maybe they were late and had to pay that extra late fee), they haven't made much more money. Yet they still convince themselves that they need to get rich this way instead of sitting down and getting "durable riches" by way of hearing the anointed Word first and getting a new spirit in them.

As a preacher I'm not going to hand you anything to make you rich. Jesus didn't go around with $1,000 bills to give to people. He set out to preach the gospel to them, and that's how they were to leave poverty behind—spiritual poverty as well as financial. You can become wealthy in your spirit, soul, and body, *and* your finances off the Word of God that you receive in your heart. Some things you just cannot get until they are preached to you.

> *"The Spirit of the Lord is upon me...to preach deliverance to the captives."*
>
> Luke 4:18 KJV

Jesus was saying in this verse that we can get delivered from sin and get right with God in our spirit through the preaching of the gospel. "It does not, indeed, 'literally' open the doors of prisons," Albert Barnes says, "but it releases the mind captive under sin; it gives comfort to the prisoner, and it will finally open all prison doors and break off all the chains of slavery [to sin]."[12]

I recall an example of this when we first started our ministry and church. We had been meeting in a school when we finally outgrew our living room. Well, the husband of one of our members had a drinking problem, but he loved to play the drums. She was trying to convince him to come to church with her, and finally she told him that if he came to church, he could play our drums, even though we were so new at the time that we didn't even have a set of drums.

So one Sunday morning this man came walking into church, drunk as he could be, with his drumsticks flaying in the air, and he said to me with slurred speech, "I am here to play your drums." As he staggered in, I told him to just sit down for a while.

Then the service began, and as I preached the Word, that man started completely changing right in the service. When I gave an altar call, he put his hands up, came forward, and joined the church to get delivered from drugs and alcohol, and he got clean from them.

After a period of time, though, he went back into his old lifestyle and would go out and get involved with drugs and alcohol again; then he would come back to church and get blasted with the Word again and get clean for a while. This back-and-forth lifestyle went on for a short period of time, until finally that man got completely delivered and set free from that alcohol and those drugs by the Word of God and began to preach and give his testimony of deliverance whenever he could.

Winning against all odds includes winning against substances like these, but you must understand that you cannot sustain yourself once delivered by the Word. You must stay in the Word. In fact, you must become totally addicted to the Word and use it as your new "substance of choice"—just change the addiction and you'll stay free.

The Set Man of God

The preaching of the Word has a great effect on our spirit, which is why it is so important where you go to church and who you listen to. We see this in the story of Moses and Joshua. When Moses and the children of Israel were near the Promised Land, God told him that soon he was going to die. Moses was concerned about the people and he asked the Lord to appoint a new leader over them who would have a positive influence on their lives.

*Then Moses spoke to the Lord, saying: "Let the Lord, **the God of the spirits of all flesh,** set a man over the congregation, who may go out before them and go in before them, who may lead them out and bring*

> *them in, that the congregation of the Lord may not be like sheep which*
> *have no shepherd." And the Lord said to Moses: "Take Joshua the son*
> *of Nun with you, a man in whom is the Spirit, and lay your hand on*
> *him...and inaugurate him.... And you shall give some of your*
> *authority to him, that all the congregation of the children of Israel*
> *may be obedient.... At his word they shall go out, and at his word*
> *they shall come in."*
>
> Numbers 27:15-21

I want you to notice verse 16—God is "the God of the spirits." That means He is "the giver of life and breath to all creatures,"[13] the God of every spirit there is. The Bible talks about "the Spirit of wisdom and understanding, the Spirit of counsel and might, the Spirit of knowledge and of the fear of the Lord" (Isa. 11:2), for example. These are all from the Holy Spirit, and God is the God of whoever has His Spirit in them. So when you are reattached to God, you can have these different "spirits of" working in your life.

Remember, your spirit is the higher part of you and it is receptive to the Holy Spirit, so while you are not *that* spirit, you have those influences of His Spirit.

Then this passage says that God set a man over the congregation, as Moses requested, a man of God who would be able to minister to the people. God is the God of all spirits and He checked out all the spirits of men and knew who He wanted to appoint as the set man over that congregation—Joshua. It had to be someone He chose because the congregation was going to be like that *set man;* they were going to be influenced by his spirit.

This was God's idea thousand of years ago, and it has not changed. Notice where the *set man* is in this passage—"over the congregation." We still need godly set men (pastors), handpicked by God, to be over our congregations (our churches)—not under the congregations, not begging the congregations, not feeling inferior to the congregations. They are to be over the congregations.

We can't pick them properly ourselves because God is the only One who is able to shine the candle of the Lord upon the inside of a set man and find whose heart has nothing but cleanness, holiness, and strength before God. He is the only One who can choose a *set man* with the power of God in his life, a *set man* who has the anointing of God, a *set man* who is prospering (in his spirit, soul, and body).

We tend to run around trying to pick churches and audition pastors and give them a trial "run" to see what they sound like first. No, we need to let God place the set man over each congregation because we need to have a set man whose spirit is clean before God. That is important because you will pick up the spirit of your set man God has assigned you to, and you will be influenced by him.

I was sitting down eating my breakfast one morning many years ago and my wife had brought me a cup of hot chocolate and some toast. We had just finished traveling all over the country with ministries and working with some of the largest churches in the nation. We were very successful in helping the vision of other set men, and I believe that God then qualified us for our own.

While sitting at breakfast that morning, the Spirit of God spoke to my heart and instructed me about the church that I was to pastor, Pacific Christian Center in Tacoma, Washington. He was setting me up right then and there. I didn't wait for anyone to audition me or give me a trial run first. My wife and I started the church right away in the living room of our home, with our two young daughters as the only congregation members. As God dealt with me about how He wanted me to pastor this church, He began to grow it, and He is still growing this ministry today.

As the Spirit of God deals with the set man He sets over a congregation, that congregation is to be like the set man in the things of God. That's why you do not want a broken set man or a depressed set man or a fearful set man or a sickly set man or a sinning set man over you at your church.

Now no one is perfect, not even a pastor set over a congregation by God. But you really want to have a strong set man over you, one who is strong in the Lord and knows how to hear His voice; one who has the "spirits of" (mentioned earlier) and is led by the Spirit of God, not a man who is always apologizing for his existence and who doesn't have a relationship with God.

The spirit of the set man (the pastor) should influence your spirit in a positive way. The thing to do is to go to church and pick up the spirit of the set man. In other words, no matter how big you are in business, he is over you; no matter how much money you have, he is over you; no matter how much political power you have, he is over you. I'm not talking about a pastor with a controlling spirit; I'm referring to going into that congregation and being willing to sit under someone God has set there whose spirit is clean and ready to influence you and lead you with godly wisdom and the Word.

That's what I mean by saying you've got to pick up the spirit of your set man. Yet people often fight with that. Some congregations want to keep the preachers poor and broke, and falsely humbled, so they can control those pastors. They do things to try to make sure they look bigger than their set man (the pastor) and to make sure they look like they have more influence than their set man. But the *set man* is to be set there by God. If he is, you and I are not to try to control him—and we're not to move him.

This whole thing of replacing a new pastor every four years because you are part of a denomination is man-made. That is not how it is supposed to be set up. God wants to set a man before every congregation who has the Spirit of the Lord on them for their benefit—*because where His Spirit is, there is liberty!*

Free in Your Deeds

There are so many lost people all over this world. Some people are so lost they don't know who they are, and they are trying to become somebody else. They may be carrying somebody else's spirit, perhaps the spirit of their old drunk uncle or some other relative. What I mean by that is, they act more like him than they do anybody else because at one time in their lives they heard people say, "You act just like your uncle," or "You look just like your uncle," or "You remind me of your uncle," and ever since they've had his attitude or spirit about them.

Other people try to marry somebody to be someone else. They don't know what in the world they are doing. They have no idea who they are, so they are trying to find themselves in relationships.

You may fit into one of these categories, but the Bible says, "Where the spirit of the Lord is, there is liberty (2 Cor. 3:17). Another word for *liberty* is *freedom*. We've been looking at what it means to have liberty in the Lord, but many people do not use the word *liberty* unless they are talking about political things. So let's talk about it a little more using the word *freedom* because once you are reattached to God's Spirit, you are free from bondage to sickness, poverty, and sin in any form.

Once you are free you will not be held back any longer in God's plan for your life, but it is going to take the Spirit of God for you to be able to get free to fulfill it.

Jesus was teaching in the temple one day when He talked about this kind of freedom in John 8:32. He said, "You shall know the truth, and the truth shall make you free." The people didn't understand that this truth forces you to be free from bondages to sin. They thought Jesus was talking about being a servant to others.

> They answered Him, "We are Abraham's descendants, and have never been in bondage to anyone. How can You say, 'You will be made free'?" Jesus answered them, "Most assuredly, I say to you, whoever commits sin is a slave of sin. And a slave does not abide in the house forever, but a son abides forever. Therefore if the Son makes you free, you shall be free indeed."
>
> John 8:33–36

I like to say that last line this way: You shall be free in your deeds, meaning you will be free not just in deeds, but in anything you are doing. If you go into business, for example, you can be free to do what you need to do. When you are trying to buy a house, you can be free. When you are raising a family, you can be free. When you are looking for more finances, you can be free. If you are looking to get your health back, you can be free. You can be free because Jesus set you free. Yet too many Christians are carrying the wrong attitude, the wrong spirit, about them—which is keeping them in bondage.

When you are born again, you are born to be a winner. So the right attitude or spirit to have is one that says you are a winner. Yet to get the victory you must deal with some things to have and maintain that attitude, and we'll be discussing them in the next few chapters. For instance, the Bible says to renew the spirit of our minds. (See Eph. 4:23.) That's talking about the way in which we think—not just *what* we think but *the way* in which we think about it. As we're going to see next, to win against all odds, we must think like a winner!

CHAPTER 4

You Are What You Think— How to Think As a Winner

I remember something that happened to me years ago when I was going through radio broadcasting school. I was young, but I had a vision to work as a radio announcer for the top station in my area. One day while attending class, one of my teachers told me, "People like you just cannot make it in radio, especially the well-known radio stations in big markets." Did I allow this man to discourage me and destroy my dream? No, this was fuel for me to work harder.

I did not believe those words and I would not allow them to penetrate my mind, for I had renewed my mind to the fact that I could succeed in my endeavor. So after graduating with honors, I got my first job at a small radio station in town, but I still had my sights on the top radio station in Seattle. It was the most popular station in the city and paid big bucks.

Most people who start out in this business have to go to a smaller market before they can reach the big-time market, but my mind was made up, and I decided to put my faith into action. So I went to that top station to meet with the program director, but it took several attempts before I finally met with him. After listening to my audition tape of a show I'd done, he kindly said that I didn't sound like a professional announcer but more like I was still in school at a little no-name station. That didn't faze me because I had a renewed mind and I knew that with training I could become what they were looking for.

Instead of giving up, I asked him if I could, on a weekly basis, bring an audition tape to him to review with me—to point out my flaws and tell me what I needed to work on. He did, and I applied everything he said. Over the next six months, I started to sound different on the station where I worked—more like the big-time announcers on the Seattle stations. That program director said the same thing at our last meeting and he finished up with, "When can you start to work for us?"

I worked there nights, so I had my days free and ended up working part-time as an instructor for the radio broadcasting school I had attended. One day my path crossed with the teacher who had said that I could not make it in this business and he asked me what station I worked for. When I told him, he couldn't believe it. He said that he had never worked for a major market radio station and asked me how in the world I got that job.

I may have not been qualified at the beginning, but I did not let that stop me because I didn't think the way my instructor wanted me to think, and I wouldn't allow his views to deter me from my vision. You see, my mind was renewed with who I am in Christ. I am a winner—and so are you.

We've seen that we are created by God and for God and that we are created in His image. We are each a spirit person, which gives us the ability to worship God in spirit and connect with Him because we are created like Him. That means your ethnicity doesn't matter or how you were born or where you were born. *You are already a winner, because God created you in His image.*

So the problem is no longer people, but your own mind—the way you think. I am not saying that you may not have to press through a lot of misconceptions in the minds of other people, but you have control over the way *you* think.

You actually think in two places—in your head and in your heart. In the Bible the Greek word for *heart* is the word "kardia," which means, "The soul or mind, as it is the fountain and seat of the thoughts, passions, desires, appetites, affections, purposes, endeavours...the middle or central or inmost part of anything."[1] Your heart is the deepest, most inner part of you, which is called the *inner man.* It's the place no one is familiar with except you and God.

Your belief is controlled in this inner part of you. You entertain thoughts with your mind, but you deal with real issues—the things that you become—from your heart. It may cross your mind to eat dog food, for instance, but it's not in your heart, so you won't eat it.

I'm not playing down the mind, because your mind is a battleground for all sorts of crazy thoughts. That's why it's very important for you to help your mind out by putting good things in it. Remember, feeding your mind with evil things will cause bad to come out of you, and feeding your mind with nonproductive, useless information will not help you either.

When a negative thought comes to you, like a thought that you are a failure, you must immediately get rid of it by replacing it with a positive, Word-based thought, such as with God's help, all things are possible. (Matt. 19:26.) Tell yourself that over and over; let the words play a continual recorded message in your mind that it is possible. Besides, God specializes in what man can't do, because He can.

If you don't do this, then you will think about the negative thought constantly and eventually it will become a stronghold that will be a part of who you are because it goes from the head to the heart (the innermost part of you). You need to guard your heart by guarding what you think, "For out of [the heart] are the issues of life" (Prov. 4:23 KJV)—but this guarding begins by taking heed to everything you hear.

Protect Your Ear Gates

In the process of losing every negative thought, you must take a look at what you are hearing. If you hear something (either positive or negative) over a short or long period of time, you will have faith for it. Sometimes it just takes one session of being in an atmosphere of words that will cause you to win or lose. It may be in an assembly of some sort or just sitting down with one person, but it is vitally important that you take heed to what you hear.

Simply put, you need to be aware of what you hear because what you hear eventually will become what you believe, and what you believe will eventually become what you think, and what you think like will eventually become what you *live* like—you will live as a winner or a loser.

Several chapters ago I mentioned that you must be born again to become a born winner, but even if you choose to become a born winner, you can still live as a loser. A person can go to heaven but still live like a beggar while on this earth, all because of what they hear on a regular basis. I'm going to give you an example to help you to understand what I'm saying.

Suppose you have two best friends, but they go to two different churches (the principle is the same for any kind of assembly, like attending college and majoring in two different areas). Say these two friends are regular churchgoing girls. One goes to a church where she is hearing words like "God loves you; God wants the best for you; you can change your life; sin will separate you from God's best, but He is a forgiving God; God wants you to prosper and be in health."

The other girl is attending a house of worship where she is hearing words like, "God will put heavy burdens on you to teach you a lesson," or "You have sinned and God is mad at you," or "Prosperity is of the devil, and sickness is God's way of getting your attention." Both girls are hearing words, but both are hearing a different message.

Faith comes by hearing, and it is safe to say that the first person in this scenario will believe that God is good, while the second person most likely will be terrified of God. So which girl do you believe will have faith that she can win in all areas of life? Of course, it's the first girl.

It is imperative to understand that we live off words we hear and respond to. You can live an unsuccessful life or a victorious life just by the words you hear regularly and believe. Do you understand why you must take heed and pay attention to what you hear, and decide if it is good or bad for you? Hearing what God has for you that is good on a regular basis will help your life in a positive way. The right faith will come, but it will come by hearing the right words and hearing the Word of God.

Let me explain it this way. While you are hearing the good news of the gospel being preached, it is hitting the atmosphere and is like a mixture of faith that is coming to you. Your heart is like a glove catching a ball (the Word) being thrown from the mouth of the minister to you, and while it's being pitched right to you, your faith is ready to catch it so that it can begin to work in your life toward victory. You can create this kind of faith atmosphere by listening to the correct teaching and preaching of the Word of God.

A winner protects their ear gates, meaning you need to be very discriminatory regarding words. Words must be compared to the solid foundation we talked about because everything you hear is not good for you. So you can't be afraid to say, "No, I do not receive these words into my life. I reject those words of failure. I will receive only words that will give me a good life." Learn to immediately analyze every word you hear and make a decision to receive them or reject them.

This is like planting seeds for a specific harvest. If you want an apple tree, you would plant apple seeds in the ground to receive a harvest of apples. Whatever type of harvest you want, that's the type of seed you would plant. In the same way, words are like seeds, and the ground is your ears, so you need to receive only words that will produce whatever kind of harvest you want in life.

You are in control of what you allow to harvest in your life, and the life you live is a totality of what you hear. Remember, what you hear is how you will think, and what you think is how you will live: "As [a man] thinketh in his heart, so is he" (Prov. 23:7 KJV). So put your foot down today, not tomorrow, and change the way you think and talk by taking control of what you hear, and you will win against all odds.

Are You Still in Egypt?

God talks often in His Word about our hearts, minds, and thoughts. For instance, in Proverbs 4:23 TEV He says, "Be careful how you think; your life is shaped by your thoughts," and He gives us a biblical account of this in Numbers 13. It paints a vivid picture of the effect that hearing the wrong words can have on people's thoughts and their lives. As you read it, you'll see why I call this the grasshopper mentality story.

God had given the children of Israel victory. He had brought them to the land that He had promised to them for many years (hence He called it the *Promised Land*). God is only as strong (to you) as His Word is, *to you*—if you put much importance, belief, and faith in God's Word, then He will become strong to you. God told us, "What I have said, that will I bring about" (Isa. 46:11 NIV), so every time you hear the Word of God, you should hear it as words to change your life.

God and His Word are one. You cannot separate the two. When we hear that God had a promised land, we are hearing that God said something, and when God says something, we ought to take note of it and believe that what He says is coming to pass. In the case of the Promised Land, some of the children of Israel had a problem with believing what God said.

When the Israelites reached the border of the Promised Land, God told them that before they entered it themselves, they were to send 12 men in first to spy out the land. These 12 spies were made up of men of the 12 tribes who lived within the camps of Israel. They were leaders of each tribe that had come out of the captivity of Egypt. God took the Israelites out of Egypt overnight, but Egypt, the place they were freed from, had not gotten out of them.

While they had lived in Egypt, they had learned the mentality of a slave. They had a mentality of being broke, of always being servants, of not ever owning a home, of not really having control of their own lives, and not having their own money. The government gave them everything.

They were government workers, but they were slaves to the government so all they knew was restriction by the control of those over them. They did not have the mentality of ownership themselves. They did not have the mentality of controlling wealth themselves. They left a place physically, but the mindset they learned, the thoughts they had, were still very much alive in them.

They were physically out of Egypt, but Egypt was still in them and they were still thinking like slaves. They were still thinking, *Somebody's going to provide for me. I'm a victim; I'm always getting beat on my back, I can't have anything, and I'm not going to own anything.*

God tried to get that mentality out of them for 40 years, but He never did. So He wouldn't allow any of them to enter into the Promised Land until all the Israelites ages 20 years and older, who had grown up in that Egyptian environment and still had that slave mentality, had died. (See Num. 14:29.) Their mentality was hard to change and even God couldn't change it.

Now, nothing is impossible with God, but He created us with a free will to choose what we believe, so He couldn't change the way they thought about being defeated and never winning—that was up to them. But they had no intention of changing. Just look at the things they thought they weren't going to have anymore.

They thought about not having enough, they thought about not being able to make it, they thought they weren't going to have water to drink, they thought they weren't going to have vegetables like they used to eat back in Egypt, they thought they weren't going to have an adequate place to stay. The problem was that they didn't understand two important truths about God: God is only as good as His Word, and His Word is good; and God (to you) is only as big as the Word you believe He is.

Let me ask you a question: How big is God to you?

Get Rid of a Grasshopper Mentality

God took the Israelites to the Promised Land and had them send 12 spies to search it out, but notice the kind of report they brought back. Ten spies returned with a negative report, and only two spies came back with a victory report. Ten of those spies thought that it was too much for them to conquer, but the other two spies said that they were well able to take the land.

Joshua and Caleb were the two spies who believed their God and His Word—and both got their victories even into their old age. You don't hear anything more about the ten unbelieving spies, but you still hear about Joshua and Caleb. You can read the book of Joshua in the Bible, you can read about Caleb in several books in the Old Testament, but who are the ten spies?

No one really hears about those ten men after Numbers 13 because people only want to hear about winners. In fact, when Caleb said, "I'm still getting my mountain," he got it (his promised land)—at the age of 85 and still full of strength! (See Josh. 14:6-13.)

I'm trying to help you to understand that if you are in the wrong environment, you cannot change because you will keep hearing that you can't, and you won't; you will keep hearing that it doesn't happen for you, and it never will—unless you know how to change your thinking to line up with the Word, not people's opinions.

I don't care what anybody tells me, when I lock my mind around something that's in line with God's Word, I'm getting it. Those things that are revealed to me by Him belong to me and to my offspring. So I put ownership on them by saying, "They're mine, in Jesus name."

Has God revealed to you that something belongs to you? You have to lock in and say, "I am a winner; I don't care what they say about me. I can do this. I can have that." You need to make a decision of who you are in Christ by thinking it and saying it. Caleb did that to get what belonged to him. Numbers 13:30 shows us that he had a giant mentality: "Then Caleb quieted the people before Moses, and said, 'Let us go up at once and take possession [of the land], *for we are well able to overcome it,*'" but not everyone believed Caleb.

The next part says: "The men who had gone up with him said, '*We* are not able to go up against the people, for they are stronger than we.' And they gave the children of Israel a bad report of the land which they had spied out, saying, 'The land through which we have gone as spies is a land that devours its inhabitants, and all the people whom we saw in it are men of great stature. There we saw the giants'" (Num. 13:31–33).

Notice what people see as important here—-what other people look like and where they come from. The ten spies were looking at the tall stature, the physical bodies, of the inhabitants of the Promised Land. God does not look at people the same way as humans look at them. God looks at the heart, but it's human nature to look first at a person's appearance.

Thank God He does not use the outward appearance for the qualifications of a winning criteria. You may be short in stature and believe you are ugly or whatever you feel are your imperfections in life, but God still has you slated for victory, not victimized living.

Notice how those ten reporters of bad news saw themselves. They reported that they saw the giants, the descendants of Anak, and said, "We were like grasshoppers in our own sight, and so we were in their sight" (v. 33). When they saw themselves as nothing, only as a grasshopper, as a victim, they became that in their mind, and their thoughts became their worst enemy. Here's the problem with the grasshopper mentality: because they thought this way about themselves, their enemy thought this way about them.

Why do we get angry at the way some people view us, when we view ourselves the same way? I believe the reason is that we do not want people to see us in a negative way, and we know that they are seeing us the way we see ourselves—as grasshoppers. How does a person change from a grasshopper mentality to a giant mentality?

The first thing is to stop blaming people for their view of you. It does not matter what anyone's opinion is of you. What's important is God's opinion of you, and He thinks only good thoughts about you: "For I know the thoughts that I think toward you, says the

Lord, thoughts of peace and not of evil, to give you a future and a hope" (Jer. 29:11).

Actually, when you learn to see yourself as a winner first, you get to the point of not caring what others think of you, including people who do not like you, because you know who you are without their opinion factored into the equation.

This is an important principle to understand: Before people saw you as a grasshopper, you saw yourself that way and, therefore, carried yourself as one. People can see through a poor self-image, which is really what that mentality is.

The second thing you can do is to notice your best attributes. If it's hard for you to judge that, ask a good friend or family member, whom you trust and know has your best interest in mind, to tell you what they believe are your best attributes. You have many good attributes, and once you know what they are, you can start thinking about these areas. Then you can look at yourself in the mirror every morning and say what you believe are your best qualities.

After you have done that, thank God for making you a winner. We will look more at what we say later, but you could say something like, "Thank You, God, that I am a winner because of You, and I'm not a loser. Now I'm ready to win again today." Believe this, know this, think this. Don't ever have time allotted in your thought process for any negative thoughts.

Be sure to put the past behind you too by not allowing yourself to meditate on the past. Instead, put your mind on the fact that you are on top, and things can go right for you.

What I'm really talking about here is renewing your mind.

Renew Your Mind Daily

When my teacher at the radio broadcasting school spoke those negative words to me, I had to decide how I was going to think. I was able to stay focused on my vision and not be deterred by his pessimism because I had kept my mind renewed.

Renewing your mind should be a daily practice. The word *renew* has a lot of meanings, but I like the ones that say, "to cause to grow up,"[2] and "to...renovate"[3] or improve. I had to grow up and improve to sound like the big boys in radio, but I could not have done it if I didn't have a renewed mind.

If you are going to think right about yourself, what kind of thoughts should you have? What do you renew your mind to? There must be a standard, a right way to think that is not considered a haughty or overinflated, puffed-up attitude. Having these attitudes would only produce pride, and pride always comes before destruction. (See Prov. 16:18.)

When you are prideful, people usually don't want to be around you. On the other hand, you don't want a weak-minded "I don't want to think too much of myself" type of attitude either. That kind of person may think they're acting in meekness, but in reality it's weakness, or having false humility instead of true humility. Where is the balance?

> *"Do not think of yourself more highly than you ought, but rather think of yourself with sober [moderate, sensible] judgment."*
>
> Romans 12:3 NIV

You should think the best about yourself—it is pivotal—but there is a measure for the way you should think. The measure of your thoughts will still remain high, because right thoughts about yourself should be based on God's Word. According to one verse He said His ways are higher than our ways, and His thoughts than our thoughts. (Isa. 55:9.) That means we can always be ascending higher in life, so we are truly a work in progress, which makes life fun. Yet it is up to us how high we go—our mind is our "limiter." If we continually renew our thoughts with God's Word, there will be no limit to how high we can go!

In the Bible we are told *how* to think and what to think *on*—which are two different processes. The word *how* means from what source and to what degree; it also means by whose help, in what manner, and for what reason and purpose.[4] Referring to our thoughts, the "source" is the Bible, the "degree" is measured only by God's higher thoughts regarding us; "by whose help" is God's help; "in what manner" is in moderation, avoiding a haughty attitude; and "for what reason and purpose" is to fulfill God's plan for our lives. So, then, what do we think on?

We are to think only on thoughts that are of the standards of God's Word. Remember, His thoughts are higher than our thoughts, so to know His thoughts we need to read the Bible. I like *The Living Bible* version of Isaiah 26:3 that says, "He will keep in perfect peace all those who trust in Him, whose thoughts turn often to the Lord!" The Word guarantees you that if your thoughts turn often to God and to what you read in the Scriptures, you will have peace that will transcend (or rise above) all human understanding.

Basically, we are to think on foundational principles—on what is true and good and right, not on what is false and bad, and wrong. We are to think on things that are pure and lovely, not on what is dirty and unloving. (See Phil. 4:8.) We are to think about what is good about others. In other words, we are to think like God. When we think like Him, we're thinking the right thoughts, and that includes what we think about ourselves.

Be determined that you are going to think no evil and speak no evil about yourself or the things you really desire in life. Believe that they will work out for your good, according to God's Word, because you love God and you are called according to His plan. (See Rom. 8:28.)

What God Calls You

Another thing—stop apologizing for your existence. You are not a mistake or a mishap. You may not be where you want to be yet, but you are on your way. Besides, a person who is always apologizing for who they are simply does not know who they really are based on the Word of God.

Start pulling yourself together now and use the part of your mind that God has given you, a great thing called an imagination, to see yourself heading to the top and not living defeated anymore.

See yourself in a new lifestyle, see yourself in a marriage that is working if you are married, see yourself with a successful single life if you are single, see yourself with the best, see yourself with the promotion or the business you desire to have, see yourself serving God in a great way. Stop looking at everybody else and what they think of you and for once really think that you can, and you will—because you are a winner right now. God sees you as a winner, and you have the right to think the same way about yourself as God thinks about you.

The psalmist David wrote, "How precious… are thy thoughts unto me, O God! how great is the sum of them! If I should count them, they are more in number than the sand" (Ps. 139:17-18 KJV), and what God calls you is a sign of what He thinks about you. Let's look at some of the things God calls us.

1. *God calls us friend.* (See John 15:15.) That's how He thinks of you—not as a servant where He is controlling you, but as a friend. A good friend will tell you only what is best for you. A good friend will be faithful to tell you the truth because they always have your best interest at heart. A good friend will stick with you through hard times; they won't leave you, but will always look for a way to help you. A good friend will make sure that it's not a give-and-take relationship, but a give-and-receive and receive-and-give mode of operation.

Now that you've seen the way a true friendship works, how do you answer this question: "Is God your best friend?"

2. *God calls us a new person.* When someone becomes a Christian, he or she becomes a brand-new person on the inside: "If any man be in Christ, he is a new creature: old things are passed away; behold, all things are become new" (2 Cor. 5:17 KJV). Physically nothing has changed, but inside, the spirit of the person has changed. Remember, you are a three-part person: body, soul, and spirit. You can relate to the physical world, the emotional world, and the spiritual world.

When you become born again, God sees you as a new person, which means the old person or the old life is over; it's gone! God is the God of a second chance—what is done is done, it's over with, and God doesn't remember it (when we confess it to Him and ask Him to forgive us). Now you must move on in the light of this knowledge. If not, the past can be the very thing that hinders you from succeeding. God has forgiven you, now forgive yourself.

3. *God calls us to be a conqueror.* Actually, in the Bible it says that you are "more" than a conqueror. (See Rom. 8:37.) A *conqueror* is a winner, and if God called you a winner, you are a winner—it doesn't matter what someone else calls you. Let me put it very straightforward to you— don't answer to any other name. For instance, if someone calls you out loud, "Hey, loser!" *don't answer!* Keep focused and make the necessary progress toward your goal.

It's important that you understand about renewing your mind because it changes your self-image—and your life.

When I decided to end my career in radio, it was hard not having fans say my name and want my autograph. It was my job to care about who liked me and who didn't. The entertainment world is all about ratings, and according to your popularity you keep your job or lose it. So I had to major on pleasing my audience. The way I thought about me was based on what other people thought. We all want people to admire us, but that is a low level of having a good self-image.

To win in life, you cannot afford to have fans or critics. It's best to be grateful for the compliments, but not take them to heart. It is also wise not to take what your critics say to heart. When I was at the smaller station, I didn't take to heart what other people would say, and while in school, no problem. But when I went to the big time, I changed the way I thought according to how people viewed me.

This was self-inflicted, and after the career was over, I had to renew the way I thought. To change my self-image I had to constantly renew the spirit of my mind, as Ephesians 4:23 AMP says, and have "a fresh mental and spiritual attitude".

If you try to hang on to your life for yourself (as I did while working at the radio station), you will lose it, but if you give up your life for God, you will find true life in Him and through Him. It's not your physical life I'm talking about but the spiritual attitude you have. Remember, you are a spirit; that is the real you. You will find who you are, what you can do, and what you have in God. That's why it's vitally important to have a fresh outlook and a fresh spiritual attitude about yourself.

Self-image or God's Image?

I'm sure you have heard the saying, "You must believe in yourself." I am not totally against this statement, but that way of thinking could very well be the problem with some people. I truly feel that we think too much about improving our *self*-image. All we think of is "self"; it's the "me, myself, and I" syndrome.

Now don't throw the book down, keep reading. I'm from the side of the cloth that believes that if a person looks only within themselves, self could lead to selfishness and emptiness. But I strongly believe that as you get to know God, you will get to know yourself.

The number one question every person has is, "Why am I here?" If you think about it, that has to do with self-image. To end the search you can locate yourself in the knowledge of God. Here's what I mean.

If my children and grandchildren want to search to find out who they really are (in the natural), at some point they will end up with me in the family lineage, because they came from me. People all over the world try to find themselves through their family tree. That's okay, but ultimately it is vanity. The truth is that God created you in His image, and as you get to know who He is, you will find who you are.

My wife, Kathy, was adopted, but she didn't find out about this until she was eighteen years old, and she didn't acquire this knowledge from her adoptive parents. She found out from a friend. You can imagine the shock and devastation she initially experienced, and after learning of this, she confronted her adopted parents.

At the time Kathy was living in California, we were only engaged, and I was living in Washington state. After her talk with her adoptive mother, Kathy gave me a call. She was crying and very hysterical. To this day I remember the conversation and her last words on the phone to me before she hung up. She said, "You don't understand," and I must admit that I didn't, being from a strong family background and growing up with both of my biological parents. But I could hear the tone of her voice and I knew in my heart that she was hurting beyond my human help.

It's been many years since that day, and Kathy still doesn't have any information regarding her birth parents. She has no knowledge of her family tree, and she most certainly had a poor self-image of herself for many years after finding out she was adopted. But today, it is just wonderful how she has blossomed into a godly woman, all because she found herself in God. God said that He would be a Father to the fatherless (Ps. 68:5), and He became her missing parents.

As you get to know God (through daily Bible reading, praying, and spending time alone with Him), you will discover things about yourself that you will like. For instance, you'll find that God has given you the power to get wealth, and that power is the God-given ability that He measured out to each one of us. We are all gifted in certain areas, and I use the word *areas* because I believe there are many areas we are good in.

Several gifts are presently in you, and probably far too many of them are dormant only because they are not being used. If you don't know what they are, you can know if you stop and listen to your heart. God is not trying to hide anything from you. It is to His advantage, your advantage, and the world's advantage for you to get on with what you are called to do. People all around you will benefit from what is already in you.

God will not pour down money from heaven, and money doesn't grow on trees. It would be great and easy to plant a tree and watch money grow on it, but the money you need will come through the abilities you use that God has given to you. He has given you the *power* to get wealth, not necessarily the wealth itself; when you use your God-given abilities, the wealth will come.

> May grace (God's favor) and peace (which is perfect well-being, all necessary good, all spiritual prosperity, and freedom from fears and agitating passions and moral conflicts) be multiplied to you in [the full, personal, precise, and correct] knowledge of God and of Jesus our Lord.

2 Peter 1:2 AMP

Hopefully, you're getting the point. Think of it like this. I believe in the God in me. Now to me that is a stronger and more powerful belief because if I believe in the God that is in me, then I believe I can do *all* things through Christ who gives me the strength. I believe I can (through God) accomplish anything that I set my heart to accomplish. With that mindset how can I not have a great self-image? My image is not based on "me" but based on the awesome God "in me."

I feel this is a better way to think, because if you just look at "self," you can find ten thousand things wrong with you; but if you don't look at "self" but to God, you will have a better outlook about yourself and life in general.

I believe you are reading this book because you have a desire for more to happen in your life, and you want the good life. So before closing this chapter, I'm going to give you four of what I call "Think Its," which are workable solutions to a poor self-image and to a better life. When you renew (make new, replace the old with the new) your thoughts in these areas, you can live a victorious life, but you must make yourself think *this* way every time you want to think your old negative way. You are replacing an old thought with a new thought—the right way to "think it."

Four "Think Its":

1. *Do not compare yourself with anyone else.*
   Think It:
   I am unique, one of a kind.

2. *God has forgiven you. (He is the God of a second opportunity.)*
   Think It:
   I'm not perfect, but forgiven.

3. *God is your best friend.* **Think It:** God is my best
friend; I have the help
I need.

4. *You are more than* **Think It:**
a conqueror. I am a winner!

You win by winning in your thoughts first. Learning to think right is healthy for you physically, emotionally, and spiritually; what you are actually doing is changing the treasure that is in your heart. By changing what is in your heart, you have the ability to change what you think starting right now—which eventually will change your entire life.

Now that you are in the process of thinking better thoughts about yourself, there is another step you need to make.

CHAPTER 5

Developing the Faith to Win— How to Believe As a Winner

What or who you believe in or put your confidence in is absolutely the most important choice you make in life. Actually, you make these decisions on a daily basis. Do you know, for instance, that you have some level of confidence in the company you work for? You believe that if you go to work, then on payday you will receive a paycheck—but why do you believe it? The reason is that your boss or someone in the human resources department *told* you that, and you believed those words.

So on Monday morning you're headed out the door, frantically trying to beat the morning traffic to get to work to faithfully put in an average of 40 hours a week, all because you believed a person who was sitting on the opposite side of the desk when you went for the last interview the day they hired you. Your faith, your trust, your confidence was in those few words you heard from the interviewer to cause you to tell all your friends and family members that you got a good job paying good money—and you haven't received one paycheck yet.

Many people, once they have been employed for a short period of time, will go out and buy a house or a new car and sign contracts promising to make payments every month for years. Think about it—people will sign a contract for a 30-year mortgage payment just because of a few words that they believed when they were hired on their job. Most people don't worry about *if* they are going to get paid; they automatically believe they will (unless they've heard some rumblings about the company's unstableness to pay their employees).

If we can put trust in mankind, who is mortal and is subject to the elements of this world and has the ability to lie, then why can't we trust God (and His Word), who is immortal and cannot lie? (See Heb. 6:18.) If we can trust the words of man, we should be able to trust the words of God which are found in the Bible.

To develop trust we must hear the Word of God daily, not just read it, the same way that on a daily basis we hear the word of man (referring to men or women). Listening to Christian tapes or CDs, and watching preachers on TV or the Internet are some of the ways to hear the Word every day; speaking the Word yourself is another important way. Hearing God's Word regularly is important because it is what builds our faith. (See Rom. 10:17.)

In the next few chapters, we are going to look at how our faith works together with our thoughts and words, and why you need this whole package to win against all odds. In order to understand how they relate to each other, you first should know what faith is, so that's where we are going to begin.

Faith is trust, confidence, belief.[1] Hebrews 11:1 paints a clear picture of faith for us, saying, "Now faith is the substance of things hoped for, the evidence of things not seen."

Notice that faith is *now*. Faith is not tomorrow; it is "now" faith in this sense that faith is something that gives reality in your mind to those things you don't yet see. It enables you to feel and act as if what you are believing for is real, or it has an influence over you the same way as if you saw it.

Faith is also substance—the substance of things that you hope for. One Greek meaning for the word *substance* is "setting under," or "support,"[2] which implies that "faith is the foundation on which all our hopes for the future are built."[3]

Another description of faith is the evidence or as one Bible commentary says, the "'demonstration': convincing proof to the believer"[4] of things that are not seen, "the soul thereby seeing what the eye cannot see."[5]

The *Amplified Bible* version of Hebrews 11:1 says that faith is your proof: "Now faith is the assurance (the confirmation, the title deed) of the things [we] hope for, being the *proof* of things [we] do not see and the conviction of their reality [faith perceiving as real fact what is not revealed to the senses]."

Overall, faith is a very powerful unseen force. It's more real than what you are believing for. The manifestation is only the by-product of your faith.

I believe people can tell when a person has faith. Faith can also gather in quantities. Faith can be measured: great faith (the faith that overcomes), little faith (tied to worrying), and shipwreck faith (you get started, but you quit). These all describe different kinds of faith and different measures of faith.

So faith can be known as a substance, and it's the only thing that I have that is the evidence of what I do not see, yet it does exist. In other words, if you ask me to show you what I have as proof of what I'm believing for, the only thing that I can show you is my faith, which is based on my belief in God.

Let's look at something else that faith is.

Faith Overcomes

First John 5:4 NIV also talks about faith, saying, "Everyone born of God overcomes the world. This is the victory that has overcome the world, even our faith." Notice that this verse doesn't say "even our love." We need love, of course, and we want to be loved, but it doesn't mention love. It says "even our faith." Faith is how we have victory in this world and win against opposition.

Many people don't want to believe they will ever need God (but that doesn't change the fact that they do). So, how then is it that faith in God brings us to victory over this world?

Bible commentators Jamieson, Fausset, and Brown explain, "The victory (where faith is) hereby is implied as having been already obtained,"[6] because Jesus overcame the world. (See John 16:33.) Our faith in Him makes us able to do the same because we have become one with Him and are filled with His Holy Spirit.[7]

Let's look at another point on the word *faith* in this verse because I want to get this applied to your heart. It talks about "our faith." That sounds almost like it's saying our faith *together,* but you have to take this and apply it personally.

When it says *our* faith, understand that you are not necessarily going to have victory in life off of someone else's faith. You are not going to make success off somebody else's belief. You are going to need to have your own faith and learn how to use it if you are going to have victory in your life. If you are going to be a winner, you need more than just "connections"—*you* must have some faith.

You don't get this faith just hanging around the right people. Faith, the Bible says, comes by hearing and then the Bible tells you what you have to hear—the Word of God. (See Rom. 10:17.)

It would be wonderful if all you had to do was to go and borrow someone's faith for a little while to get what you want or need in the same way you go to a neighbor's house to borrow a couple of eggs. However, after awhile they will want you to learn how to go to the store to get your own eggs, and there will come a time when you will need to get your own money to go and buy your own eggs at the store. That is true for your faith too.

There must come a point when you will need your own faith, but know that it costs something—your time. Daily Bible reading, prayer, being alone with God and receiving wisdom and knowledge from His Spirit is time well spent. I call it *faith dues* to get what you desire in life.

A person can't just sit at home, watch TV, eat bonbons, and want somebody else to get their faith for them. They need to make an effort to do what's necessary to hear the Word of God, to receive the good news of what they can do, and use their faith for what they desire.

You may say, "Well, all I need is more money." It doesn't necessarily require money. Money is not the substance of things hoped for. See, money can't bring faith, but faith can bring money. If you don't have any money, you definitely need some faith. Likewise, healing can't bring faith, but faith can bring healing. A good marriage can't bring faith, but faith can bring a good marriage.

Faith is what you use to get what you need and what you hope for in your life.

Look at it this way. There are things a person can acquire in life, but how did they acquire those things? Was it by dishonest gain or hurting others to reach their goal? Was it by leaving God out and doing their own thing, following their own plan? If so, they are still not winners (because they are out of His will for their life)—but you can win by your faith.

So what is this faith I am talking about? It is not only the substance of things hoped for and the evidence of things not seen, but it is the victory that overcomes—you overcome all odds by your faith.

Here's another fact about faith.

Faith Is a Personal Possession

What I mean by that is, you are responsible for how much faith you have and how it works. Many people sit back and literally eat peanuts while they are flying on jet airplane trips. Perhaps it is landing even in bad weather conditions, yet they have faith that it will land safely and simply do not think anything about it.

You don't even know who the two pilots are who are sitting in the cockpit flying the plane. As far as you know, there could be two monkeys in there doing the flying. Yet these two pilots are in there landing that plane in that bad weather, and you are sitting back in your seat eating your peanuts as if everything is fine.

The pilots are simply watching two crosshatch instruments used in bad weather landings for instrument landings. They are watching a crosshatch of which way they are factoring, left or right, or up or down, to be able to meet that cross right in the middle. That crosshatch instrument is telling them exactly that they are on the guide slope and localizer instruments, while it's storming and raining and they cannot see even one or two miles in front of them.

However, in their mind they can see (they believe) that they are going to be landing at the airport soon, as the runway (they believe) will appear in their windshield. They are looking at their instruments and watching that localizer to locate them and the guide slope to take them up or down, and it has to be a crosshatch at all times. If it goes down they go down, if it goes up they go up, if it goes left they go left, and if it goes right they go right. That is what they are using their faith for—those instruments.

They may not be Christians, but they are using faith, while you are sitting back eating peanuts while monkeys (for all you know) are flying the 737 jetliner. You've got faith and they have faith that those instruments are telling them where to bring all those 200 passengers. They land on the ground and think nothing of it. People do it every day all day all over the world. They have faith; they just put their faith in their instruments.

Generally speaking, every person on planet earth uses faith—faith for what will work or faith for what will not work. But the Word of God should be your localizer. It should be your guide slope. Get off course according to the Word of God and you may start going down. Get off of the Scriptures and you might get a little too high up. Get off of the Word and you may go off to the right and hit a tree, or on the other side you might hit a building. The Word of God is what keeps you on course.

You have to put your faith in God's Word as your localizer, as your guide slope, to bring you in to land and receive the blessings of God. We use our faith like that all the time in all kinds of different things. For instance, if you stop the right person and ask for directions, they will give you complete details on how to get to where you're going. They will tell you which sidewalk, what color the sidewalk is, how many trees there are along the way. People just like to tell you details.

All you did was ask a complete stranger where is so and so street, and you believe what they say. You look for the driveway, you look for the brown car, and you look for the mailbox with the dent on the side because they told you. How much more should you believe God? All He asks you to do is to believe what He tells you in His Word and He will take you to the address called Blessings Boulevard.

The Starting Place of Faith

When the Bible says that faith is the substance of things hoped for, that tells me we need to be hoping for something. This is why mediocrity is not to be a part of a winning life of faith. If you are living a life where everything just goes along and you don't have anything you are hoping for, then you don't have any hope in front of you. It is not a sin to hope for better. You can have hope and use your faith for your hope to materialize.

Gas heaters have what is called a pilot light, which is a tiny flicker of fire used to ignite a big flame and cause the entire house to be heated. I call *hope* the pilot light. At least we can make ourselves get the pilot light of hope on within us about what we desire to have come to pass and hope that something better is possible. We may not have put on the full gas source to the flickering flame of hope yet, but at least we can be ready with our hope for the things to come.

If your pilot light wick is wet (if you have no hope), you will never ignite the fuel of faith. This is where you have to make yourself stay optimistic about the future because you have God in your life. It is important for you to stay excited with at least hope; then faith has a starting place in you.

Hearing and reading the Word of God will help you to stay positive and hopeful. Then you can add your faith, which will be your confession (or words you speak) of what you believe you receive and of Scriptures, and watch your desires ignite before your eyes.

When you have faith, you have hope, and hope is your expectation. People with no hope are desperate people. Hope is necessary first, and then you need faith to bring what you are expecting to come to pass. Your faith for a period of time is the only evidence of what you are believing for. Here's a simple scenario to help you understand.

If a man goes to court and stands before the judge, and another person stands before the judge and says, "I accuse this man of saying something he does not have," the judge could say to the person who is being accused, "Present your evidence that you do have this thing you are believing for." So that man brings to the court his faith based on the Word of God. That is his evidence.

In the court of God, that's all you need. Your faith, based on the Word of God, is the only evidence that stands up in the court of God. Faith is trust, and faith comes by believing what God said in His Word about you. That is why I highly recommend that your trust be placed in the solid foundation of the Word.

In general, people want a solid foundation in their lives. I believe deep inside every human being is the need for love and the need for stability. Everything in our world changes, nothing stays the same—except the Bible. It has been tested and people have tried to destroy it, but it still stands strong as the Word of God to man.

You can look at the Scriptures as God's blueprint for your life. Your faith and my faith will be in someone (even if that someone is ourselves) or some type of thing because we were created to trust—but in whom do we trust, or what do we trust in to help us through this life?

Throughout generations, mankind has tried trusting in other people and things, but anyone or anything other than God and His Word will always eventually fade away and no longer exist. If my faith must be in something, I believe it's wise to place it only in the One who made me and said that He has the manual on my entire life. (See Ps. 139:16.)

Expressing Faith

So far you have learned that faith is substance, evidence, trust, a possession, and the victory that overcomes the world; but did you know that faith is expressed through words? You will lose or win by what you continually say in life: "I believed and therefore I spoke" (2 Cor. 4:13) is a fundamental truth and a foundation you can chose to build your life upon.

We saw earlier that what you give your thoughts to is important, "As he thinks in his heart, so is he" (Prov. 23:7). If you habitually think on something, it becomes a part of who you are. Thoughts will cross your mind, but that does not make them a part of you unless you regularly think on those thoughts and set your attention to them to carry them out. If you do, then the thoughts move from your head (or mind) into your heart (not the pumping device inside of you, but the real person you are—your spirit).

Do you know that your heart thinks? Some people regard this just as your conscience, but according to the Bible, the heart represents the spirit. That's why I keep emphasizing changing how you think—not as you think in your head, but as you think in your heart—because it can change you and the way you live, but that's not all. Your heart or spirit also hears.

In another passage of the Bible, Jesus said, "He who has ears to hear, let him hear!" (Matt. 11:15). He wasn't talking about hearing just with your ears but hearing with your heart, like opening your heart up and hearing what I'm saying now, because your spirit man has ears.

Something else your heart does may surprise you—you talk in your heart.

Have you ever talked to yourself? Most likely there are times you've said something inside of you, but did not say it verbally where someone could hear you. For instance, have you ever told a person, "This sure is good food; please give me some more," but all along your heart was saying, *I don't like this food?* You said something with your mouth that wasn't really in your heart. You just talked from your head.

What thoughts are you thinking about that are in a well inside of you? What thoughts are in the secret place of your heart?

Whatever thoughts are inside of you will come out of you eventually, because "Whatever is in your heart determines what you say." (Matt. 12:34 NLT). Remembering that words are seeds, what seeds are you planting? Or I could ask you this question a different way: What are you confessing?

Your confession is an expression of your faith. You declare your faith by what you say, good or bad. You can have faith for the negative things in life or the positive things in life; either way you will eat from the fruit of your lips. You must say it before you live it, but you will think it before you say it. Basically, if you think you can, you will; if you think you can't, you won't—because you'll say it.

Maybe you want to live a prosperous life. If so, you must think it first and then you will say it. You will declare your faith (plant good seed) if that is what's inside of you. You could say something like, "I believe I am prosperous" or "I believe I will succeed." It starts out with confession. You say it with your mouth, preaching to yourself, to hear it with your ears so that you will believe it in your heart (the spirit person).

Jesus instructed us on confession in the following verse.

"For assuredly, I say to you, whoever says to this mountain, 'Be removed and be cast into the sea,' and does not doubt in his heart, but believes that those things he says will be done, he will have whatever he says."

Mark 11:23

This will work if you just don't let doubt enter in. Jesus wasn't talking about removing Mount Rushmore but about being victorious over big problems, problems that seem like the size of a Mount Rushmore. There's no limit to how many good things can happen for us if we just won't doubt in our heart.

Most people start out strong in faith, believing they can succeed, but then a negative, doubtful thought comes to them and fear takes over. They allow themselves to believe it just won't work. Or they allow their mind to think on all of the obstacles they are facing, and their thoughts become what they believe in their heart. Notice this verse talks about doubting in your heart, not in your mind. The first place that doubt will come to is in your mind, but then the doubt will proceed to travel to your heart.

Remember, once it is in your heart it will come out of your mouth. Then you will start saying what will not work. For this reason, you must short-circuit negative thoughts before they enter your heart, because once they are in there, they become your life.

So when negative thoughts come, like you won't succeed, you must learn how to cast them down. When I say cast them down, I simply mean that you must learn to immediately reject the thoughts and replace them with winning thoughts.

It's easy to tell you what to do, but it will take some effort on your part to actually do it. Can you see why it is very important to train our mind how to think? Yet we train our body but often forget to train, or retrain, our mind.

Your mind can be your worst enemy or your best asset, but either way it affects your heart so you must learn not only to renew your mind but to arrest your heart. Make a decision that from the heart you are going to be as God is, and the body will follow. Choose to get your heart thinking right and speaking right to get the process going the right way.

That is the process God used when He spoke the worlds into existence and when He created mankind. What's so powerful is that He gave us a gift of using the same principle that He used— to say something and receive what we say.

CHAPTER 6

Faith Speaks—
How to Talk As a Winner

Living by faith is to be a lifestyle. This is the way you live—by faith. Most importantly, God is pleased, but while our faith pleases Him, there's another reason for His pleasure with our faith.

> *By faith we understand that the worlds were framed by the word of God, so that the things which are seen were not made of things which are visible.*
>
> Hebrews 11:3

If you can see it, it was made by faith and spoken words. In fact, you and I were made by this process. God said, "Let Us make man in Our image" (Gen. 1:26), and the Bible says that He created man from dirt. (See Gen. 2:7.) Then God said, "It is not good that man should be alone; I will make him a helper comparable to him" (v. 18), and God created woman out of man.

God knew what He was going to do—He said it, and it came to pass. So then we too have the ability (the gift) to say things that line up with the Word, and they can come to pass because we are made in God's image. God created everything by His words and because we were created in His image, He gets pleased when He sees us follow Him by speaking things into existence. It's not a weird concept; it's the way people live every day without realizing it—they live off of words, good or bad.

Death and life are in the power of the tongue, according to Proverbs 18:21. In a simple way of looking at it, death represents bad things in life, and life represents what would be good. Right now if you were to take a quick inventory of your life, I'm sure you would find that your life is really made up of words that you spoke over and over again—not just one time, but habitually speaking the same thing because your faith will speak.

Living this way is what pleases God because He gets pleased when you use His Word—when you put your faith in His Word, speak His Word, and believe that you receive even when it doesn't look like you have it. That's faith in action, and it's how you win against the odds.

You go by what you believe, not what you see, and you say what you desire until your words are stronger than the circumstances you are facing. What you are doing is walking by faith, not by sight. (See 2 Cor. 5:7.) Here's another part of putting your faith into action.

Have you ever heard of other successful people saying that they were never born with a silver spoon in their mouth? When you get right down to it, they are saying they had to work hard for the success they achieved. My take on this is that you must put your feet to your faith. You can think it, say it, and have faith for it—then you must do it. But I believe there needs to be a balance.

You must be willing to compensate for time lost with your family, extra money that must be spent, and especially time missed with your spouse. Take mental note that every sacrifice made is temporary; you need to make that clear in your mind. If not, you will develop new habits that will not necessarily be healthy habits. I'll give you an example.

Years ago I was studying to become a pilot. I had faith that I could get my license, and I spoke what I was believing for, but I also had to take action. When I was studying for different types of ratings for flying, I had to put in many hours. These hours took the place of some of the hours I would have spent with my wife.

The type of material I had to study at times was overwhelming. I had to reassure her (and myself) that this was only temporary. Instead of looking at the tunnel, I had to look at the light at the end of the tunnel. I had to look long-range, but I had to get my wife to see it too. Oh, I had faith for everything I had to accomplish—I was saying that I was going to make it, and I wasn't planning on losing my family or wife in the process—but I still had work to do. So I had to learn how to prioritize success.

I had to make some small sacrifices with my time and my money to have the success I desired, but I had to keep in balance with my wife and children.

What is your faith saying? Are you having faith for good things or bad things by what you are saying? Are you having faith for things working or not working in your life by what you are saying? Are you having faith for winning against all odds by what you are saying? Are you putting the faith you are speaking into action?

The way you live is a result of words you have spoken.

It isn't easy to speak past what you may be feeling or seeing—it may be hard to look past all the bills, for instance—but faith will speak that those bills are paid and then you can take the needed actions on your part. The part you can do you do; the impossible things you can't do, you trust that God will work out, and He will. That's faith in action.

Here's what we've learned about faith so far. Faith will speak—and faith will speak as if the thing is already done. Yet it's not just saying something, but doing something, because if you really believe you already have it, your faith will take action and you will do things physically to demonstrate you have faith for your hope.

Suppose you are hoping for a new job with better benefits. Faith will say that you believe you receive this new job with better benefits. You believe you have it before you see it. You say you have won against the opposition before the result is actually manifested. Then you go out and apply for the new job, standing in faith on the Word of God, and believing that the job is yours. It may look impossible in the natural, but this is how you win against all odds.

God Specializes in the Impossible

All things are possible with God. In fact, your impossibilities are His specialties. I have seen this work many times in my own life.

I remember once when I had a $50,000 debt to pay, and I just did not have the money at the time to pay it. This was about the same time that a family member needed to borrow $500 from me. I loaned the money, but later, in my heart I felt that I needed to call this person up and tell them that they were released from this debt. The Bible actually gives a principle that worked in this situation.

In the book of Matthew, Jesus was teaching His disciples to pray, and in that prayer they were taught to ask God to forgive their debts as they forgave those who were indebted to them. (See v. 6:12.) I took this passage literally as financial debt, not a sin debt (the Greek word for *debt* has both meanings[1]), and when I released this person from paying me back, God worked on my behalf. I got a call the following week from the person I owed, and the first thing he said to me was that he was having a good day, and I came to his mind. In the conversation, he told me not to concern myself with the $50,000 I owed him.

God worked out an impossible situation because I felt that He was telling me to release someone of their debt to me, and then God touched the heart of the man I owed to release me of the $50,000 debt. How would you like someone to call you up because they were having a good day and release you of your debt you owed them?

It was an impossible situation. I just didn't have the money at the time to pay that debt, which was owed at the end of the week, but I won against that impossible odd because I released $500, knowing that something good was going to happen for me. I believed that God was telling me to release the person who owed me the money, and if I obeyed God, I knew He would work on my behalf.

I had faith in God's Word, so I said to Him, "Forgive me of my debt, as I forgive the debt that (the name of the person) owes me." Then I just started thanking God for the results by saying that I believed that my debts were cancelled. I know this doesn't make sense, but it makes faith.

Winning begins with words from your own mouth. It is not strange that I would say from your own mouth, because what you say is important, but not necessarily what other people say about you. What others say about you can have a strong impression on your life, but only if you believe the words, either negative or positive, and you start to repeat them from your own mouth. If you take those words to heart, their words can influence you. If not, then those words will never germinate in your heart, and it will be like those words fell on stony ground.

I encourage you to stop right now and say this boldly, not weakly: "I am a victor. I am a winner. I win against all odds, not just some odds, but all odds." You may be thinking, *This feels too bold and arrogant acting.* I know it does, but you must think this way first, and then you must say it. What are you going to do, wait for someone else to give their opinion of you and then start thinking about what they say and repeat it? No, you need to control the thinking around you by thinking first!

People try many things in life, yet why is it so hard to try it God's way? I needed help, and God already had my help available by hearing His Word and speaking the Word from my mouth, because faith speaks. But I had to have faith for myself. When you have faith, you'll know what to say, which is necessary because faith is an action, and the first action of your faith is speaking what you believe you have.

If you do the things we've been discussing, especially building up your faith with God's Word, speaking your faith will not be a problem. I'm not talking about speaking what you don't have or what you think you will have, but speaking what you believe you have.

You must be definite when you talk to win. You cannot speak any words of doubt or hesitation. Doubt is a strong force, but not stronger than faith, especially if your faith is in the right place—God. Remember, with God all things are possible, and He specializes in impossibilities. It may be a challenge when you are in the middle of a trial or negative situation, but what is impossible for us to do, God can do.

Controlling Doubt

You know by now that your mind really is the place where you lose or win. There is a lot to process in your thoughts on a daily basis to decide what you will believe and retain or what you will reject and discard. You can't go through life wearing earplugs for your ears so you can't hear anything or eye guards for your eyes so you can't see anything or a muzzle for your mouth so you can't talk to anyone. A person could wear them, but it would look very silly; and even with all of them in place, you still would have to deal with your thoughts.

An undisciplined thought life will give you an undisciplined life. You may lose in a fistfight and you may lose in a word fight, but in the battlefield of your mind, you don't have to lose. You can win if you fight the good fight of faith, or what some call a faith fight. What is a faith fight?

Instead of boxing gloves, you use the Word of God, which is considered your weapon and is "mighty through God to the pulling down of strong holds" (2 Cor. 10:4 KJV). The strongholds are negative thoughts, and these thoughts will lead you into doubt. When in doubt you become uncertain about your past, present, and future; actually, it's a lack of faith in God and in yourself. But when you take captive every thought and compare it to truth, something that never changes, you can be guaranteed that you will win against all odds.

I believe that what God said is reliable truth. The Bible is the same yesterday, today, and forever. (See Heb. 13:8.) It's been relied upon from generation to generation. Great men and women have found peace just by reading it. I have personally found it to be the source of my strength and the answer book to my own questions of life itself. That's why I encourage you to read it daily. Start with the book of Proverbs; it will give you insight into life and how to handle it.

You are responsible for your own mind just as you are responsible for your own faith. What you think, and what you think about long enough, will determine what you do. Faith can move big problems, but you have to believe this. Believing starts with your thoughts and works itself down to your heart, which is why it's so important to learn how to take control of your mind—so you won't get into doubt. We've already looked at some characteristics of doubt, but I want to give you some ways to fight doubt that have to do with what you say:

1. Decide not to succumb to any doubts at all. Doubts will come, but fight doubts with faith by saying that you will overcome and win against all odds.

2. Decide immediately that you will not give up your desire. Be passionate about what you believe you should do in this life. Hold on to your purpose and see it fulfilled. Ask God to give you insight and wisdom on how to do it, and watch Him step in and help you.

3. Find a passage from the Bible that you can confess, and say over and over again until you receive what you are believing for. Remember, faith comes by hearing and hearing by the Word of God, even if you're the one speaking the Word. For instance, you could say, "With God all things are possible, so I am winning against all odds."

Mark 11:23 tells you that you can say to the mountain, the big problem facing you, to be removed. Just talk to it, whatever it is. Maybe it is a lack of money, or the lack of opportunity. You can tell lack to leave you and the lack of opportunity to be removed from you, and believe that it is done according to what you say. If you don't say it, who will? Stop saying what you don't want in your life, and start saying what you do want to come into your life.

Speak Power-filled Words

Unfortunately, our mind thinks a lot of crazy thoughts that left unchecked can cause defeat. You can learn how to handle doubts by getting rid of them. You do this by inserting words that have already been tried and tested and that are based upon the Word of God. Here are some faith confessions you can speak over your life, but I encourage you to read the Bible and find more for yourself.

"For God has not given me the spirit of fear, but of power and of love and of a sound mind" (2 Tim. 1:7);

"I will prosper and be in health as my soul prospers" (3 John 2);

"When my ways please the Lord, He will make my enemies at peace with me" (Prov. 16:7);

"I am more than a conqueror"; "I can do all things through Christ who strengthens me" (Rom. 8:37; Phil. 4:13);

"Only goodness and mercy shall follow me all the days of my life" (Ps. 23:6).

Isn't this wonderful that we do not have to come up with words on our own that do not work? We have the Scriptures to find words that are full of power and will bring life to those who believe in them. In the Bible we can find words that have been tested and settled in heaven; words that are a shield, words that are sharper than any two-edged sword; and most importantly, words that are eternal. To help you better understand the power of words or power behind words, let's look at it this way.

Suppose that a captain in the military tells a sergeant to stand at attention. What do you think that sergeant will do? Yes, that person will stand at attention and even salute the captain. Yet why does this sergeant even listen to this captain, and why does the captain have the right to make such a command?

I'm sure you know the answer—the captain has delegated power handed down from a higher authority due to the position and the chain of command. So the words from this captain are paid attention to by those who are under his or her authority. If those words are not listened to, that sergeant will get into serious trouble.

Another good example is from Matthew 8 regarding a Roman centurion's servant who was sick. This soldier went to Jesus pleading with Him to heal his servant, and Jesus replied to the centurion, "I will come and heal him" (v. 7). Just look at the power of words here in verse 8. The centurion answered, "Lord, I am not worthy that You should come under my roof [in other words, don't come to my house]. *But only speak a word, and my servant will be healed.*"

Notice what Jesus said when He heard these words, "Assuredly, I say to you, I have not found such great faith...." (v. 10). The centurion understood the power of words, especially words that Jesus spoke, and Jesus said that this man had great faith—great faith just because he believed that words could be spoken from the location he was at to the location of his servant.

You can see from this story that words are not limited to distance, because they are spirit in nature. The tongue has the power of life and death, and it represents the words that you speak from your own mouth—you can speak words that will build your life or destroy your life.

So God's words spoken from your mouth and backed by your faith in them will shape the life you desire. His words are spirit and they are life. (See John 6:63.) They are full of power; unstoppable by any evil force.

When Jesus was led into the wilderness to be tempted of the devil, He did not succumb to the temptations because He used the Word of God as His weapon. (See Matt. 4.) What will you use to win when you are faced with opposition? What will you say when you want to quit? What are you saying now?

Words are used by people every day and that is the reason why sometimes there is no value placed on them. Some people just run at the mouth. They just talk and talk about what is not happening, how they are in so much debt, or they can't pay their bills—"I just don't have enough; I'm broke." Or they say that one day they will get sick and die just like their uncle, or they will never make it in life. These are the type of words that will keep a person in debt and broke, or open the door to sickness, maybe even the same sickness that the uncle had.

"The worlds were framed [or created] by the word of God," Hebrews 11:3 tells us. What are you creating? It will take some practice to start to speak words of life, especially if you have only been speaking negative words over your life. You may feel uncomfortable at first, and most likely it will sound foreign to you to speak words that will bring life, but this is only because you habitually have been speaking words that were bringing you death.

You may see this as positive speaking and negative speaking, but it is so much more. These are power-filled words backed by heaven and its angels.

> *"Bless the Lord, you His angels, who excel in strength, who do His word, heeding the voice of His word."*
>
> Psalm 103:20

When you allow the Word of God to come from your mouth, you have just released the power of God and the angels to work on your behalf. You may not quote the Word verbatim, but as you continually put His words in your heart and out of your mouth, you will have good success. I'm going to give you two examples, because this is vitally important for the rest of your life.

You Decide Your Destination

In Mark 9:23 we read, "If you can believe, all things are possible to him who believes." Based on this verse you could say, regarding your situation in life, "This is possible; I can do this." Or you could speak out 2 Timothy 1:7 so it can relate to any challenge you may be facing, "I do not have fear; I have power, love, and a sound mind." Your confession of faith becomes that you have power, love, and a sound mind, not a troubled or a senile mind.

I have heard people say about themselves that they are going crazy or that they are a dumbbell or stupid. There are times I just listen and will not say a word back to them. But there are other times I will stop them by saying, "Don't say that about yourself." If someone says idle words about me, I am very quick with a response by saying to them that I don't receive those words.

Notice that I just mentioned the word *idle*. Every nonoperative word is an idle word. The angels of God will not fulfill idle words, but the Bible says that one day we will be accountable for every idle word. (See Matt. 12:36.) Idle words are empty words, but the devil will make sure these words are carried out. I am not talking about words used occasionally; I'm talking about the words you speak habitually, over a period of time—those will manifest.

A man's heart determines his speech. A good man's speech reveals the rich treasures within him.

Matthew 12:34,35 TLB

So whatever treasure is stored up in your heart that is what will come forth from your mouth. I said all this to take you to the point of *saying* what you have learned to think. As you continue to think the four "Think Its" I gave you earlier (and hopefully you will not stop at these four and no more), you will automatically say them because they will be stored up thoughts in your heart.

Just for practice I want you to say what you have been thinking. I'll call this, so you can remember, the four "Say Its." Now say these four confessions out loud so you can hear yourself.

Say It #1: I am unique, one of a kind.

Say It #2: I'm not perfect, but forgiven.

Say It #3: God, You're my best friend. Thank You for helping me.

Say It #4: I am a winner.

You can paint a pretty or an ugly picture on a canvas with a paintbrush, and you can paint a pretty life or an ugly life on the canvas of your heart with your words. Remember that death and life are in the power of your tongue and that you decide the destination you want to arrive at, good or bad.

You may be thinking, *What if I had parents or teachers who said I was stupid and will never make it in life? Am I just doomed for life?* Definitely no! You will need to stop thinking those thoughts that were submitted to you, and start to think the way God wants you to think—what He says about you in His Word. It will take work on your part, but stay with it and you will reap a good harvest.

Ultimately, it is your responsibility for the outcome of your life. It is *your* tongue that holds the power of death or life, not the tongue of another person. Do you recall that childhood saying, "Sticks and stones will break my bones, but words will never hurt me"? I will say yes and amen to this *if* you don't allow other people's words to hurt you, but your words you speak out of your own mouth will hurt or help you.

Say what you want; speak Mark 11:23 and tell the mountains (the odds) that are against you to leave. Remember, that verse says you can get whatever you say if you do not doubt in your heart. If doubt does come your way, then you must fight the good fight of faith by saying what you believe that you have, even if you don't feel like it.

The bottom line is, you need to speak your faith. Remember, "I believe and therefore I speak" (2 Cor. 4:13 TLB). In other words, what you believe you speak, trusting God that He will help bring it to pass.

So stop thinking whatever will be will be and whatever is going to happen is going to happen. Start to speak your life into victory because this is how you can live as a winner. Begin now and be determined that you are going to live this way for the rest of your life.

CHAPTER 7

"See" It Before You See It— How to See to Win, Part 1

Have you ever wanted to quit something because it did not look like it was working? Have you ever received a notice in writing and you read the words "Not qualified"? Have you ever heard someone tell you that you just don't measure up? Have you ever discovered a lump on your body and believed you were going to die?

What I have just brought to your attention is the ability you have to relate to the elements of this world by your senses. In my examples above I used sight, hearing, and touch, but as you know, you have five senses in all—hearing, smelling, seeing, touching, and tasting. Thank God for these abilities; without them it would be harder to function in the world in which we live. But I believe that we have a sixth sense—what I call the faith sense—and I'm going to make a statement about it that may startle you: You must learn to walk by faith and not by sight.

We have seen what faith is and that you can win when you speak faith-based words. What I want you to learn about faith in this chapter is how to walk by what you "see" on the inside of you, not what you physically see. I am not saying that you walk around blindfolded and that your physical sight is not important, but I am going to show you how to take control of your five senses and walk by your sixth sense in order to win against all odds.

Before I do, I want you to understand that as we walk by faith and not by sight, we must learn to develop this sixth sense. This faith sense I am talking about will "see" things before they manifest in the natural realm. By that, of course, I mean see them in faith. Let's look at a biblical example of this.

In the Bible God told Joshua (he was the leader after Moses) that He was going to allow him to conquer the city of Jericho, but the gates of Jericho were kept tightly shut. Yet God said to Joshua, "See, I have given Jericho...into your hands" (Josh. 6:2 AMP). Notice, God did not say that He would *give* Jericho but that He had *already given* the city into Joshua's hands. I believe that *see* in this verse represents the sixth sense, or the faith sense. God wasn't going to do it; it was already accomplished by faith.

Physically Joshua did not yet have the city, but by faith he already had the victory. Now the only thing he had to do was to put works with his faith, because faith without works is dead. For this reason, God told Joshua to march around the city only one time for six days, and then on the seventh day, to march around the city seven times. At that time the priests would then blow the trumpets, the Israelites would shout, and the city walls would come down. After Joshua followed God, Joshua got the manifestation of what he saw by faith. (See v. 20.)

Faith is another way of seeing things. You must see what you are believing for in your heart first before you will see it in the physical. When you begin this process of walking in faith, you must carry out what it is in your heart to do by putting works to your faith. In a previous chapter we called this faith in action. The steps that you need to take will come as you submit your time to God in prayer for His guidance and direction.

I know this may sound a little strange to you perhaps, but start seeing the things you desire in your heart before they come to you in the physical. I'm seeing those kinds of things all the time; so should you. This is how I built a church building worth millions of dollars. I saw it by faith before I saw it in the physical. Then I paid an architect to draw what I saw so that others could see what I had already seen in my heart.

Basically, others who will run with your vision will walk by sight at first, but you must continue to walk by faith. So the reality of seeing the vision is more real to you than it will be to others, just because you can "see it" in your mind's eye without physically seeing it.

I wanted to be as close as I could to the property I had acquired for the building to allow people who needed to run with the vision to see progress, so a building was temporarily rented in viewing range of the property. The building that I was going to build would be a house of worship and I had to get other people to see it like I was seeing it as much as possible.

It's very important to understand that you can't make your dream come true without the help of other people. But the joy of this is the fact that while your dream is coming to pass, the dream of others can come to pass along with yours. It goes back to seed-time and harvest—people who plant into your dream and reap the harvest of their own dream.

So as I saw by faith different things that were needed to start and complete this project, I got others to see by faith with me.

The first thing I saw was a tractor. The property I had acquired needed to be excavated before a building could be built on it. I saw by faith tractors on the property clearing the land, and then I would tell others what I saw. But in the physical, there were not any tractors on the property yet. I did not tell people what I was not seeing by sight; I was telling them what I saw by faith. I was using my sixth sense.

After saying this several times to members of my church, they started to say the same things. What was very precious is that little children who were a part of the Sunday school classes started to talk about tractors too. The Sunday school teachers were teaching them to see tractors by faith. Then I started to say that I was hearing the tractors, and I continued to say that until tractors were physically on the grounds.

The amazing thing was that I hadn't finished getting the financing. I did not have the millions of dollars manifested at the time to build this new building. We had only just closed on the property and we hadn't even gotten our construction company signed off on the bottom line ready to do much of anything. Yet, I chose to walk by faith, and I saw and heard tractors working on the property.

The children in Sunday school grabbed hold of this faith concept and they would run around telling their parents, "We hear the tractors too," as they pointed out to their mom or dad where our acreage was for our new church facilities. At that point they had more faith that the tractors were starting to run on the property than most of the adults.

Eventually, the building I saw by faith got built. This is a very simple act of faith.

Built to 'See and Say'

If faith is what causes us to have victory, then we need to understand, comprehend, and study how faith relates to the five senses more fully. Faith is not an imaginary thing. Faith is more real than anything material because faith is how the material thing gets there. Remember, "Faith is the substance of things hoped for, the evidence of things not seen" (Heb. 11:1). We looked at substance, hope, and evidence in a previous chapter. Now we're going to deal with seeing—what you see or how you see things by faith.

I showed you earlier that the word *evidence* is the ground for belief or proof. I submit to you that we really can't get very far into faith without learning to have the ability to see things in our minds that we don't physically see. In other words, you have to "see" it before you see it. You have to see yourself with it before you have it. You have to see it inside of you first before you see it outside. After you "see" it, you've got to say it—you have to see and say.

When my daughters were little, they used to have a toy called a See n' Say. To play with it they had to turn the dial to the different animal pictures or to the ABC's and then pull the string. If you turned the dial to where the picture of the dog is, for instance, and pulled the string, it would say "This is a dog—woof, woof." It's a See n' Say, so whatever you see, it would say it. That's the way you need to be. You need to see what you desire by faith and say you have it by faith.

Many times when I have been hearing the Word of God, I'll start saying, "Oh, I see it." Have you ever done that? Actually, you are saying that you see something good happening, and hope is being brought into your heart. The will to go on because you are going to make it is being built inside of you. Yet this can work in reverse if you are hearing negative things. It may build fear in you, and you may start to see the negative things happening. The reason is that you are built to be a "see and say," and what you say all the time can come to pass.

That's why it is very important for you to feed your heart and soul on good things and not bad things. Humanly speaking, if you hear it (bad or good news) on a continual basis, you will "see" it, and if you see it, you will say it and then you will have it. Let me give you some practical ways to "see" it before you actually see it.

1. Is It God's Will?

You must know that it is the will of God for you to possess whatever it is you desire. Why go around seeing things that are not for you to see? I will give you a good example; it will be direct and to the point, but you will understand the principle behind it, and that is what's important.

Say you have an eye for someone else's spouse (when I mean an eye, I'm talking about your desire to have someone's spouse). This may be a desire, but it is not from God. Actually, from the Bible standpoint it is considered lusting, which is of the world. We all must learn how to overcome the lust of the eyes, the lust of the flesh, and the pride of life (1 John 2:16), which is not from God but from man (speaking of our society).

Why would God break up someone's marriage and take the children (if they had any) through the devastating effect of a divorce? In many ways, divorce has become very acceptable in our society, with Christians and non-Christians alike, but that doesn't make the awful effects go away. So the very first thing that is important is to know that what you desire is the will of God for you. When you know that you know, and your knowing knows, it is easier to stay put until your desire comes to pass.

A good way to get to know all that is yours or belongs to you is by reading daily the Word of God. I have mentioned this several times already, but it bears repeating because there you will find everything you need to give you the knowledge of what belongs to you. But to sum it all up in just a few words, good success and abundant life belong to you. All good gifts come from above (James 1:17); for this reason, all good things belong to you.

Many Bible scholars have said that there are over 30,000 promises in the Bible. I haven't counted them all myself, but I do know they are numerous. I have personally obtained many promises for my life and found that the dividends are wonderful. Not only do I benefit, but also my family and everyone who comes in contact with me benefits. That is one promise you will find in the Book—you are blessed to be a blessing.

Let's look at another way to "see" it before you see it that is sure to help you to see what you desire come to pass.

2. Pray Simple, Effective Prayers

It's exciting and rewarding to know what you were born to do here on this earth, how to solve complex questions and problems, winning when things are against you, and how to obtain peace of mind, which every human being wants and searches for daily. Prayer is the key to your success for all of these and for many other wonderful benefits that can be derived from it.

I must admit that this is an area of little interest to many people because it is strange to them to pray to someone you can't see. They think that if you can't see the person, how do you know that they heard You? Besides, they wonder, *Who do we pray to?*; *When do we pray?*; and simply put, *How do we pray?* I'm going to answer these legitimate questions in a moment, but let me ask you a question first.

Why do we call the nation to pray mainly when a catastrophe happens? Why will the president of the United States and news anchors and your neighbor and people in general ask everyone to pray when devastation takes place in our world? Why does it seem as if no one has a problem saying "let's pray" when trouble occurs? Then when the trouble subsides, we generally go back to our old ways, and prayer is the furthest thing from many people's minds. This is my own observation, but I don't believe I'm far off in thinking it.

The point is, prayer is simple and easy to do, but very effective. I will explain three types of prayers here (but there are others)—the prayer of petition, the prayer of agreement, and the prayer of thanksgiving—and briefly explain them for your knowledge and the benefit you can receive from them as you win against all odds. Before I do, I'm going to go back and answer the simple questions mentioned earlier.

Who do we pray to? Prayer should be directed to no one but God. He is omnipotent, having unlimited power; He is all-powerful. God is omnipresent; He is present in all places at the same time. And God is omniscient, having infinite knowledge; knowing all things. Why not pray to a God like this? He can help you with anything, anytime and anywhere. That means you can pray anytime and anyplace because God is there.

A designated time of prayer is the most valuable time of my life on a daily basis. I look forward to starting my day off that way. I may spend one hour praying, and I never go to prayer without a pen and a notepad. Why not? I am waiting to receive answers to my questions, direction for my day and life, and wisdom to accomplish my goals.

After I address God, then I start talking to Him as if I was talking to a close friend. I try not to hide anything from Him, knowing that He knows it anyhow. But at times, when you know that you blew it, it is hard even to tell God about it. I just expose my heart to Him knowing that He cares for me. I ask Him for wisdom and direction in things that I don't know how to handle. At times I will ask Him for things that I desire to have.

In closing the prayer, I end with the name of Jesus. It's like signing a check. A check is no good unless the authorized person signs it; it's the same principle when we pray.

We are encouraged to exercise first thing in the morning, but I also encourage you to pray in the morning. Yet prayer doesn't have to be limited to the mornings. You can pray in the afternoon and evening too, or any other time of day or night—and prayer isn't limited to one type of prayer. Here are several ways you can pray to help you to see what you're believing for come to pass.

The prayer of petition.

This is one that most people do on a regular basis. This prayer is centered on asking God for specific things. It is a request to God. There are some people who believe that it is wrong to ask God for anything. They believe that God is sovereign, which means that He is superior to all others, and He is, but that doesn't disqualify you from praying this type of prayer.

You are created by God, and He doesn't take offense to you praying to Him and asking for things that you desire in life. Because He is sovereign, and we are under His care, He understands our human frailty. The short version of all this is that we need help and God knows it—and we want things!

In many places in the Bible, God tells us to ask Him. In Luke 11:9, for example, He says, "Ask, and it will be given to you; seek, and you will find; knock, and it will be opened to you." Isn't this good news? We ask and He answers; we seek or search for and we find; we knock and it shall be opened. So there is work to do— *prayer* is an action, *seeking* is an action, and *knocking* is an action.

You can see that we have our part in the winning department and God has His. Too many times we just think that people and even God owe us something, but there is work we must do, and praying is a form of work. It takes some effort to pray, especially when you don't want to.

Hasn't it ever been in your heart to pray and you just didn't feel like it or you were just too tired or (excuse me) but too lazy to go pray? We can all use a thousand reasons not to do something that takes effort to do. But remember, I will only tell you what works, and prayer works!

I have done it for many years and I have found it to be effective only in my winning against the many odds I came face-to-face with. I can tell you of countless stories of praying and getting answers that turned out for my good. For example, I can recall praying for my spouse. Actually, at the time we were not married, and I needed to know if this was the wife for me.

Now don't think that I have gone off on the deep end. I know this may sound foreign, but I was only 18 years old (that's pretty young to think about marriage), but I was thinking, and thinking hard. I needed to know about this because I was raised that marriage was for a lifetime, and I had better get the right wife. So I prayed and simply asked God if the girl I was dating should be my wife.

Big question for an 18-year-old, but after asking this question, I had a vision. And in the vision I saw my wife (who was my girlfriend at the time), and I saw her holding a child (who looked just like our son when he was a baby), and I saw myself preaching. I only asked God about the wife, but He showed me a baby and me preaching. The baby was great, but preaching was out of the question. I had no desire to do that.

After I had the vision, I knew it was right and I married my wife, Kathy, after three years of dating. We had three children (including the son I saw), and eventually, after many years in the radio and television broadcasting field, I pursued what was in my heart—preaching. All of this came out of one prayer on one night in an old upper room in a Baptist church. As young as I was, I was compelled to pray.

When you sense that urge to pray, go for it. Just do it. But even if you don't feel the urge, just do it anyhow. You will make much progress in your life. It will comfort you and give you peace of mind. Don't you need peace?

Now getting back to the question of how do you know that God will hear you. The way you can know is that He said He would.

"Now this is the confidence that we have in Him, that if we ask anything according to His will, He hears us. And if we know that He hears us, whatever we ask, we know that we have the petitions that we have asked of Him."

1 John 5:14-15

Sounds like a bull's-eye to me, and you know what a bull's-eye is—a direct hit. According to this passage, your prayer did not hit the ceiling of your room, but it went straight to heaven. It is your assurance that you will have what you asked for if you have asked according to God's will (which is the Word of God).

See how important it is to know what is in the Bible? I mentioned to you earlier that you need to read the Bible daily to know what belongs to you. In there are promises for you. One thing I know for sure is that you were destined to have good success. Health is yours, wealth is yours, emotional healing is yours, peace is yours, wisdom is yours, understanding is yours, knowledge is yours, good success is yours, and on and on the list continues.

What a wonderful life is waiting for you if you take the time to pray! So don't be afraid to go to God and ask Him for your heart's desires—and expect to see them come to pass. Now let's look at another way to pray.

The Prayer of Agreement.

This prayer takes at least two or more people coming together to pray. I suggest that you use just one other person, because the more people you add the more you must be certain that they agree with you for whatever you desire to have. I like to pray with my wife if I desire to pray a prayer of agreement because I know her, and I know that she wants the best for me and for both of us.

Agreement with the person you are praying with is vitally important. You can't pray with just anyone.

Let's say you needed a drink of water at work and you went to the water cooler. One of your co-workers was standing there getting a drink himself and you walked up to the cooler to get your drink and said, "Hey, Joe, agree with me that I get that new position they just opened up in the company," even though you knew that Joe applied for it as well.

Joe looks at you, and says, "I will," just because he doesn't want to be rude, but he goes away and says to himself, *Why would he ask me to agree with him to get the position if he knows that I had just applied for it? He has the nerve to come to me to ask me to agree with him.*

When you want to use the prayer of agreement, which is a powerful prayer, you must ask these questions of yourself:

1. Is that person of like-minded faith? Do they believe like you? For instance, if you were sick, do they believe like you that you can be well again?

2. Does that person want the best for you?

3. Can they continue to believe with you until you get the results you are believing for, or will they after a period of time tell you to just give up; there's no hope?

Allow me to mention two more forms of prayer that will help you tremendously as well to "see" before you see—the prayer of thanksgiving and praying in the Spirit. Many people don't think of the prayer of thanksgiving as a prayer, but it is. Others don't understand the term or how to pray in the Spirit, but both types of prayers are valuable keys to your success. I encourage you to add them to your life. Let's look at praying in the Spirit first.

Praying in the Spirit.

I will touch on this kind of prayer very briefly, not that it is the least important; I believe that it is the fastest way to reach heaven with our petitions. It is praying with a heavenly language, unknown to me but known to God. Yet this type of prayer is accepted by some Christians and rejected by others, so I am going to give you various Scriptures on it for your own study time of the Word of God.

I encourage you to search and ask God about praying in the Spirit yourself, because I believe you will agree with me that this is the most effective tool to get direction and the help you need. With this in mind, search these truths out:

> "Likewise the Spirit also helps in our weaknesses. For we do not know what we should pray for as we ought, but the Spirit Himself makes intercession for us with groanings which cannot be uttered. Now He who searches the hearts knows what the mind of the Spirit is, because He makes intercession for the saints according to the will of God. And we know that all things work together for good to those who love God, to those who are the called according to His purpose."
>
> Romans 8:26–28

Notice that all things will work together for your good as you practice this type of prayer.

> "If you then, being evil, know how to give good gifts to your children, how much more will your heavenly Father give the Holy Spirit to those who ask Him!"
>
> Luke 11:13

All you need to do is ask God for this gift to pray this way.

"But you, beloved, [build] yourselves up on your most holy faith, praying in the Holy Spirit."

Jude 1:20

When you pray this way, you will build yourself up in your inner man, which means you will make progress and rise like an edifice, higher and higher. There are many times you will need this "building up" as you go forward working toward the dream that's in your heart, and winning against all odds.

Now let's visit the last type of prayer I'm going to talk about.

The Prayer of Thanksgiving.

This type of prayer should be seen as a lifestyle, something you practice all the time, not just after you prayed. Being grateful or being thankful will cause your life to flourish in more ways than one. It will propel your vision to move faster in the right direction.

One of the reasons the children of Israel wandered in the wilderness for forty years was because of their mouths. They murmured and complained about their living conditions and their leader, Moses. Unfortunately because of that they didn't partake of the land that was promised to them; at least not the people who were over twenty years of age.

It's a sad case to think that they were delivered from a bad situation in Egypt and were on their way to a better land with a bright future, but they got impatient and discouraged and sabotaged their own success. Being thankful opens the door for many opportunities, but it is the most important key to use to see the vision you have in your heart physically take place before you in your life.

Are you starting to "see" things? Remember, I'm only telling you what will work. Now let's go to another important area that will help you to "see" it before you see it.

3. Write Down Your Vision

The desire you have in your heart will take place, the Bible says, but you must first write it down. (See Hab. 2:2–3.) If you don't, it will only be wishful thinking. A *wish* is just something you want; a *vision* is something seen by other than normal sight. When you have a vision, you see it first inside of you, but you still must do something. God says that you must write it down, because writing it down:

- Imprints it on your mind and makes it more clear to you;

- Reduces it "to a certainty" and preserves it "safe and pure";

- Allows you to review it after it is fulfilled, and compare the event with what you have written.[1]

So when you write the vision down, then it becomes a vision that is in the process of being fulfilled. In the world system, we understand this as a business plan.

If you have a business in mind, to get financial backing and other people involved you must have what is called a business plan. In this plan you must present the vision of your potential business in writing for others to read. The outcome you want is for a financial institution to get excited enough to put money into it. Another goal is for other people you want involved to "run" with it. What is the mission of your potential company? Writing it down in a business plan lets them know.

I'm not asking you to give a detailed business plan, I'm just saying that you need to write down your vision in a simple way that you can understand and that others who might read it can understand. It is not a business plan (but a business plan can come from it); it's a vision that is in your heart from God and is expressed on paper in a very simple way.

> *"Write the vision and make it plain on tablets, that he may run who reads it. For the vision is yet for an appointed time; but at the end it will speak, and it will not lie. Though it tarries, wait for it; because it will surely come, it will not tarry."*
>
> Habakkuk 2:2,3

Write your vision down and be sure to make it plain (or clear). Then, make sure you declare it and speak of it on a regular basis. Every day, find ways to speak about what *will* happen, not what *may* happen. What may happen is not faith, only wishful thinking. You must have confidence that what you desire will take place, so speak of it as though it has already happened.

> *"[Speak of] those things which do not exist as though they did."*
>
> Romans 4:17

Others will hear of it and some will run with you. You'll have some who might laugh at you and even tell you that it may not work, but there will be many who will see what you see and want to be a part of it. So go ahead and get comfortable in declaring your vision from the rooftop until you see the manifestation of what you believe. After you write it down, then put it in a place where you can review it periodically.

These are all successful steps for you to take to make things happen in your life. People mistakenly believe that things just happen accidentally that will give you the success you want.

Successful people who are winning in life and walking in their dream had to work to get things moving toward the goal. Remember, faith without works is dead. Yes, you must believe, but you must do many things to physically see what you see in your heart—and a very important step is to first write it down and start talking about it.

Once you write down your vision and start to talk about it as often as you can, then you must wait for it. One dictionary defines the word *wait* as "To rest in expectation and patience."[2] *Patience* is another word you will become familiar with while waiting to see your vision manifest.

Patience is a wonderful virtue. It is a great asset for you to have. When you are waiting or being patient, you are doing so while being busy as a bee. You're working toward your goal daily, doing at least one thing. Every day look to add another piece to the puzzle. This is a good way of looking at it—the bigger the vision, the more pieces you have.

People often start out with a smaller puzzle that is less challenging and then move on to something that is more challenging. But whatever is being put together, every piece must fit. It's not the size of the puzzle, it's that every piece of the puzzle must fit, small or big.

Your child may be putting together a puzzle that has only 20 pieces while you are putting together a puzzle that has 1,000 pieces, but the approach is the same—pieces must fit together. That's the life of a winner. They will continue to find the pieces that fit—and the bigger the vision, the more complex it is and the smaller the pieces. A winner will not give up but will keep trying to find the right piece until the puzzle is complete.

A winner may work on it several days or weeks or even longer, but they will come back to it and finish. The only difference between a winner and a loser is that a winner will continue to make progress against all odds, and a loser will quit when challenges arise. Oh, they may not quit at the first sign of resistance, but eventually they do give up and throw in the towel.

Now, don't feel bad if you gave up a dream once before. By your reading this book, I know that you are not a loser. A loser is not a person who gives up; a loser is a person who gives up and never tries again.

I detest the word *loser,* so I'll just use the word *defeated.* You can get defeated at the game, but just don't stop playing. Get back in the ring of life and try again, and keep trying until you win— because eventually you will if you don't quit trying.

Building Your Dream

When you write your vision down, not only is it like a business plan, it's like a blueprint—ready for you to build from it. I understand this very well. I told you earlier how we built our church building worth several million dollars. During the construction I decided to work through the entire process acting like a general contractor.

The very first thing I did after renting a building in view of the property we were going to build on was to hire an architect to put in print the type of building I saw. He came up with a conceptional drawing, but it was not for me to look at because I had the vision in my heart for the type of building I desired to build. The drawing was for other people to view so they could see what I was seeing.

I saw it in my heart, but they had to see it in living color to inspire them to want to run with the vision.

Remember, you need people to help you achieve the things that are in your heart. Really, we can't do much of anything successfully by ourselves, but it's not just about getting people to help you with your vision. Any God-given vision will help other people to fulfill their own vision. It is a reciprocal thing. So the drawing was an important step to have as an example for all to see and to talk about.

I talked about this building to so many people, and this is a very important principle—I had to talk for the vision until the thing I desired came to pass, and then it talked for itself. The vision will speak when it has manifested, but until then, you need to do the talking to get people excited and to stay excited through the whole process. You must be very confident about what you desire to do and know that it will happen.

A house sat on the land that the building was to be built on, but that land had something else on it—the biggest bull I have ever seen. The bull made it difficult for me to walk the land to see what we had purchased, but once it was removed, I was able to do that and visualize the building on it. You can see the land from a main highway in my city, so sometimes I would drive on the highway and look over to our land and from that point of view also visualize the building being there.

See your vision from every angle of life. Picture in your mind the impact it will make in your own life and the lives of others. I used to declare that one day people would drive that freeway and see this building, and people now are doing just that.

Before we could build, we had to clear the land. In other words, we had to tear down, root out, and then build. Sometimes that's exactly what you must do with your life—get rid of things that are holding your vision captive. Let me make this clear. I am not talking about your marriage if you are married. Yet I do understand that some spouses may not support the vision of their spouse.

You must be strong to succeed against the odds. Just use every negative situation as a stepping-stone, not a setback. What you do with negativity will be your road to success or setbacks or total failure. When people told me something could not be done, I never gave up; I just saw another way to do it.

The old adage, if there is a will there is a way, has some truth to it. The Bible says, "With God all things are possible" (Matt. 19:26). Personally, I have found God as a God of impossibilities. Clear your life of negative words you may say about yourself. Take a full inventory of you—not your spouse or your relatives or friends—just you. Anything that needs changing, just do it because there is work ahead of you.

It took engineers, surveyors, contractors, laborers, and so many other people to work on this building project. To top all this, there were many types of permits that were needed, including a building permit. So much paperwork, so much time, so many people, so much money—all to fulfill what was in my heart.

You must understand what I am saying. If you desire to do big things in life, you must be willing to put the time into it, get people involved in it, and put money into it. But remember, with a God-given vision comes provision.

My wife and I sacrificed many things during the actual building process. We knew we had a pearl of great price and we were willing to give up a few luxuries to see this dream come to pass. What are you willing to sacrifice for your dream to manifest? You may have to put in many hours so you will have to sacrifice some sleep. You may have to put in a lot of time, so you may have to sacrifice a few extra hours away from home. What are you willing to do?

Of course, there is a balancing act so every other thing in your life that is important doesn't fall apart. But I would be remiss in my duties by not telling you the truth. There is work to be done to see your dream become reality, and you must be determined to beat the odds.

There are countless stories I could tell you of odds I had to beat, and of people who did not believe in my God-given vision. Some were even family members, which was really tough. But when people criticize you, that is not the time to quit; that's the time to push forward. That is the time to keep your vision before you, seeing the end results.

God says that He makes known the end from the beginning. (See Isa.46:10 NIV.) Another Bible translation says that God declares the end and the result from the beginning. (KJV.) If He gets the results He gets, then we too have the license to do the same thing. We too can declare the end from the beginning. I started doing this by talking about being in the building and using it.

Sometimes people want to know my secret to success. I have had other businesspeople stop by or call asking me how I built such a building. This is one way that I did it. I started to talk about the end results at the beginning. I saw myself and people in the building before it was finished. I refused to get anxious or worried, and I could have done both.

Though your vision tarries, wait for it; if it delays, just keep working at it; never give up, because it will surely be seen. That's a promise from God, and He doesn't lie.

Resist Temptation

One more thing: Don't succumb to temptation. Now, I'm sure you are wondering what that has to do with your vision. When most people see or hear the word *temptation,* immediately they think of sexual things. But you can be tempted in many areas, including immorality. Since we are all tempted one way or another, we must understand that it's what we do with the temptation that will determine the result of the matter.

Being tempted is one thing; what we do or don't do with it is what's important.

You do not have to submit to any temptation that would bring you dishonor or disgrace or keep you from having the results you want in life. To help you, in the next chapter I am going to give you a few ways to overcome a temptation (I didn't say it's easy, but it's possible if you desire to).

CHAPTER 8

"See" It Before You See It— How to See to Win, Part 2

I remember years ago, when I was in my early twenties, my wife and I were building our first house (the one I mentioned earlier). My brother had built himself a house and suggested to me that since I liked a certain type of house I should just build it. I had a successful career and lots of money, and my wife and I were both young; but I always liked nice cars and big houses, and I thought the suggestion was a great idea.

I did not know anything about building so I had to depend on my brother for help. I got many referrals from him and started the process. To make this story short, everything was going great, the construction had started, and we were on our way soon to moving into our new house. But in the process of time, I found out that the builder was not paying the subcontractors as I had thought. I was paying the construction company I had hired, as different things were being completed, but they were not paying out to their subs.

Eventually, liens were being attached to the house and workers wanted their money. Everything was at a standstill, the house

wasn't finished, bills were not paid, and I entered into the temptation to fear—and boy, are you talking about fear!

Fear is definitely a tormentor, and it is an enemy to faith. I
could not sleep and I could not eat. It was like I was in a daze. I
would go by the house and just walk the yard. It was on a very
large acreage, and the only thing I could do was walk the grounds,
praying about what I needed to do. It was during one of those
walks that I decided to put a stop to fear.

The first step I took was to pray. I needed some answers, but
most importantly, I needed peace in the midst of what seemed to
be a no-way-out situation. I soon received that peace, and I got
some answers. Eventually the house was finished and we moved in.

As I mentioned earlier, we did end up losing that house a short
time later due to my disobedience to God, but I was young at the
time and I learned from my mistakes. I also grew in my relationship with God and began to learn what I am sharing with you in
this book.

Fear will try to grip you in many ways. It could be fear in the
areas of not having enough money, not having enough education,
a fear of telling someone about your vision, or a fear of taking the
first step toward your vision. People sometimes have fear of being
successful. They start to feel guilty of the influence they're having
and the money they are making.

Some people have actually sabotaged their own success
because of these reasons and many more. The fear of success or
the unknown is a powerful negative force. But most people must
fight the temptation to fear that will enter at the onset of starting
something new. Or once started, fear may try to grip your heart to
quit when you start to encounter resistance.

What will you do if fear presents itself to you? Will you submit your mind to it or will you be determined that you will not allow it to rule you?

Two ways to fight fear are by praying and by getting knowledge of the situation you are in. We've seen that the Bible says (and God is saying this), "My people perish for a lack of knowledge" (Hos. 4:6). That simply means that you will not succeed in your endeavors if you have a lack of knowledge in those areas. Fear will start to diminish when you start to understand some things that you need to know about what you're doing or going through.

I started to gain some knowledge for myself when I realized that I could not depend on my brother any longer. Besides, he didn't have any answer for the dilemma I was in. I had never built a house before, and I went on a search for the knowledge I should have acquired from the beginning.

You need to pray and you need some knowledge for whatever task you are embarking upon: "Yes, beg for knowledge, plead for insight. Look for it as hard as you would for silver or some hidden treasure" (Prov. 2:3 TEV). With prayer and knowledge, I have gone forward in many other real estate adventures since that first one, and all with success. Oh, I still had to fight the temptation to fear, but I learned how to became a winner.

Handling Disappointments

This is another area that can affect how you "see" it (your dreams and visions) before you see it. Everyone has been disappointed in one way or another, and at times has disappointed someone. How do we handle being disappointed? I can recall working on some real estate transactions in the past, and I worked so hard at negotiation and the amount of paperwork to fill out to get to the last hurdle, yet the transaction fell through. Can you relate to that?

Maybe you faced a similar situation because the seller decided not to sell that property at the last minute. What a heart-sinker. Or perhaps your 16-year-old daughter came to you and told you she was pregnant. You want to throw your hands up and say life is cruel. Or you've believed for something for a very long time and you don't see it happening. There is a skill you must possess and that is the skill to endure or be persistent.

The word *endure* refers to holding up under pain or fatigue; it is to stand. To be *persistent* is to continue or to be diligent. In order to win against all odds, you must master these things. You must endure and be very persistent when disappointment arrives at your door. Let me tell you something that was so disappointing personally, and how I got the victory over it very quickly.

I had started a church and after six months I wanted to have a building of our own. I looked in the city I was in and found an old building complex that was once a large grocery chain store and a few other businesses. Currently, it had one space available in this complex, which was a restaurant. So I believed for the best and talked to the owner, and he gave me the freedom to move in with only a three-month stay.

The space was abandoned and a mess. It looked like the previous tenants must have had a big party and just got up and left. It was so dirty and smelly, but I saw a lot of potential. A visionary is one who can see past what's in front of them.

I took some of the church members with me to look at it and they thought I was crazy because the inside of the space was so ugly. It was, but I saw a diamond in the making. So we moved in and God gave us favor with the owner—we ended up staying close to ten years, with an agreement to purchase. During that time we put thousands and thousands of dollars into remodeling the building and took over another space as we continued to grow in membership.

Eventually I decided to get the property rezoned, with the owner's approval, for a church; but the purchase never became reality. Another group of people from ten other organizations came together and were able to convince the owner to sell to them. I remodeled only two spaces; it had about four spaces total, but it gave a vision to these other people who wanted to use it for the same purpose that I was using it for.

After all those years, it did not help that I put a lot of money into remodeling the building and rezoning the use of it, making the building saleable. Neither did it help that I thought I had a good relationship with the owner. It was only the church members and me against the owner and this large group. I felt like David against the giant, Goliath. I only had a slingshot, not a javelin—which is about 8½ feet long.

While away on a weekend trip, my wife and I got the news about the sale of the building. We returned to town to find out that what we heard was true; the building was sold right out from under us—so we thought. I say "so we thought," because God gave me a vision to buy, sell, and then build a new building.

For ten years prior to this, I had been praying for land in a certain part of the city because one day I wanted to build a church building right next to the freeway. I could see it on the inside of me, even though there was nothing on the land yet. A person with a vision will have a long-range plan as well as short-range plans. Once back in town I called a man I respected who had built multi-million-dollar buildings and paid them all off. He was a winner, and he was my mentor.

Actually I called to get some pity from this man, but after telling him my story, do you know what he said? "God has something better for you." I did not want to hear this response, but I valued the words from this man, knowing that he is a man of high character. In the natural I wanted pity, but I am thankful I did not get it. Those words had life in them. I received the words and put a smile on my face, held my head up, and got busy.

I also received the words from my wife saying that she wanted a brand-new building this time, no more fixer-uppers. With all this in mind, along with the vision God had given me ten years prior to build next to a freeway, I turned to my wife and said, "Let's go find the land." The rest is now history.

We found the land, we built a brand-new, state–of-the-art building right next to one of the busiest freeways in the city, and God got so much glory. Oh, I still had other giants to fight during construction, but the fight was well worth it. In the process, I had to learn some life lessons, which I will list in a moment, but even God experienced disappointment.

The Old Testament tells how God regretted that He had made mankind; it grieved His heart. (See Gen. 6:6.) God was so disappointed that man had reached such a height of sin, which had spread far and wide on the earth, that He took drastic measures to clean the slate and start over. Yet in the midst of His disappointment, He still saw something good (in this case, someone good), and that was Noah. God saved Noah and his entire family from the flood that He sent to destroy the people He had created.

After the water receded, Noah worshiped God and God made a covenant with him that He would never again cut off the human race by flooding the earth. God set the rainbow in the cloud, and it was and still is a sign of the covenant between God and mankind. (Gen. 9:16-17.)

After a rain shower, we still see God's promise at work. But I want to point out the fact that God was disappointed, yet in the middle of the disappointment He saw good. I'm telling you to look for something good when you get disappointed. There is something good right before your eyes, and if you look for it, you will find it. Let's take those two examples I gave earlier.

If a real estate transaction falls through, there is more great real estate out there, so continue to look for it. If your 16-year-old daughter got pregnant out of wedlock, yes, you no doubt would be disappointed in the fact that she made a bad decision to have a sexual relationship outside of marriage. Yes, it would be a change for her and your family; it would take some adjustment and many things to work out—but the baby has nothing to do with all that.

Once that baby arrives, he or she should receive much love and care from everyone involved. It's also time for restoration. The daughter and the family and everyone else who is involved must be restored. How soon you want restoration to begin is up to you.

The point is that we can't allow disappointments to rob us from the joy that can break through if we just sit down and pray so we can find the good that is somewhere in the whole situation, just waiting to be located. If you choose not to pray, then you won't find what is good, and you will not succeed in winning against the odds—or in this case, winning against disappointments.

Here are two most valuable life lessons that I have learned, which I believe will be helpful to you in continuing to see it before you see it:

1. *You must know for certain that God will help you bring to pass whatever you really believe He gave you to fulfill in life.* So, keep your mind fixed on the big picture (the dream) you have in your heart. Don't allow any person (giants) to discourage you from reaching your destiny, because no one can stop you. If God is for you, who can ever be against you? Read Romans 8:31-39 and you will also find out that you are more than a conqueror.

2. *You can't hold any bitterness against anyone and expect to move forward.* I had to forgive and release that group of people who bought the building because I had a problem with how it was done. I moved on, and God took care of the rest. He will fight your battles if you get your hands off the situation. God always wins, and He wins big. So let go of an ex-spouse, or a former boss, or anyone else who has disappointed you, and determine to move on. Besides, God has something better for you!

Take a Time-Out

Now that you have been reading this book for a period of time, allow me to introduce you to something else to think about as you learn how to "see" it in order to see it. Life itself can be tough, but you can be tougher—when you are born again and have the Spirit of God in you. We live in a world in which nothing is certain—nothing except God, of course. We may face tough situations, but tough people last, tough situations don't.

For this reason I am going to get more into the Bible here and be strong in my approach. I believe that you are ready for a stronger message now that you have already learned many life skills in the previous chapters, and I truly feel that what I'm about to share with you is going to provoke you to see much more coming into your life.

So allow me to be to you your life coach and help you to move into another stage you must enter to become a winner. Are you ready to get challenged to go to a higher level? Let's proceed.

> *"Though by this time you ought to be teachers, you need someone to teach you again the first principles of the oracles of God [which means things spoken of God]; and you have come to need milk and not solid food."*

> Hebrews 5:12

The writer of this passage begins with a phrase that sums up the heart of this section: "By this time," meaning it's been long enough at this level. By this time you should have it; you ought to see changes in your life. Let me illustrate what I mean. You could say, "By this time, instead of sitting in the 5th grade for the seventh time, you should be in the 12th grade tutoring 5th graders."

See, instead of pacifying yourself with excuses why your life hasn't changed, you need to look at your life and say, *I ought to see some changes in my life in some kind of way by now. I ought to be living a little differently.* This could pertain to many areas, such as "We ought to have a marriage that's a little better than this," or "I ought to be single with a life, not without a life and needing to depend on another person." I mean, after a while you have to say some "ought to's" to yourself.

To be a winner, you must come to the point of growing past just seeing with your own sight and start seeing things that cannot be seen with the natural sight. I'm talking about believing beyond your dreams, for impossible things to be possible—but that's not all. When you get the impossible, then you ought to be teaching or coaching other people. By then things should be happening. You should start seeing yourself with victory so you can help someone else get his or her victory.

Maybe at this time you are still working on you, but have a vision now that you will use your success to help someone reach his or her success. That is good, but you must first take a look at where you are and honestly ask yourself, *Am I ready to teach someone else, or am I still repeating the same mistakes over and over again?*

The hardest thing a person will have to do in life is to give themselves a "time-out" from life and reevaluate what they have learned and where they have made mistakes. Have you learned from your mistakes or are you still making the same ones? Admitting your mistakes can be one of the biggest success steps you will take. The healing process will take place when you can admit your mistakes to someone else and have them pray for you as you pray for them. There is healing for your soul and restoration.

I like the synonyms for *restoration*: rebuilt, revived, mended, rested, and fresh. Just think, you will be rebuilt where you are torn down, revived where you are weary, mended where you are broken, rested where you are stressed out, refreshed where you have been dry. If you want to experience that kind of healing and restoration, there are many absolutes that you need to make now in your life that will help you settle some issues once and for all and stop making the same mistakes.

For instance, you could say to yourself, *I will not marry just any man or any woman. I will wait for the best, the one God has for me.* Or maybe by this time you should be saying, *I will not be so emotional about everything that comes my way. I will use prayer and knowledge to get me through this. I will make a decision that I will not succumb to fear anymore.*

Perhaps you should say, *I know too much. I have the knowledge to stop failing at the same things in life. I will stop going through the same mistakes. I will learn from them and move on so that I can teach someone else.*

How do you reach this point of having an unlimited source of information that will always cause you to win in life and help others? You must become *skilled.*

Gospel Milk or Strong Meat?

*Everyone who partakes only of milk [here's the problem] is **unskilled** in the word of righteousness, for he [or she] is a [baby].*

Hebrews 5:13

This verse is talking about being unskilled in the word of righteousness, or the Gospel, which is a doctrine of the righteousness of God, not of our own righteousness. We feed on the Word, spiritually speaking. The Bible has food for both the skilled and the unskilled in the word of righteousness.

In the same way we go through different stages of growth in the natural—from baby to adult—we need to grow spiritually too. As baby Christians who are unskilled in the things of God, feeding on the milk of the Word makes us strong in our spirit and renews our mind to think like God thinks. When we become full age (mature Christians), we are skilled but must feed on the meat of the Word.

Matthew Henry calls this "gospel milk and strong meat" and explains, "It is good to be babes in Christ, but not always to continue in that childish state; we should endeavor to pass the infant state; we should always remain in malice children, but in understanding we should grow up to a manly maturity."[1] Growing into a mature Christian is necessary to help us "distinguish between what is pleasing and what is provoking to God, between what is helpful and what is hurtful to our own souls."[2] This happens as we feed on the Word.

So the word of righteousness (or the Gospel) is highly important to our success. Once again, we should confess or say what God has already said about us—that's the word of righteousness, which works best by being in right standing with God. We can say that we have a winning spirit in us, because we are now born again with the Spirit of God inside of us. That makes us in right standing with God; we are not an enemy of God, but a friend of God.

Humanly speaking, when we think of the word *righteousness,* we tend to think of it as simply doing what is right—and it is important to do right. Your integrity is a virtue that I'm sure you believe is valuable.

What is more important to you—honor or dishonor, or gaining the whole world (putting success before morals) and losing your soul (your life figuratively or literally speaking)? Sounds pretty straight and to the point, but by all means we should not have a questionable character. I like the passage of the Bible that talks on this and asks that question to every person:

"What do you benefit if you gain the whole world but lose your own soul?

Mark 8:36 NLT

Is money more important to you or building a solid character? I believe you would answer building a solid character, and you would be right—but you can have money *and* a solid character. You can be rich and yet not filthy, but rich and clean. A good wholesome lifestyle should also be a legacy to leave your children. That should settle many decisions you must make in the course of your life.

When the odds are against you, what will you do to make sure you keep honor in your life? Will you compromise your values? Of course, no matter how much we try, we still cannot be righteous on our own merits—our righteousness must be of God. (See Isa. 54:17.)

When we are saved by grace, Ephesians 2:8 says, we exchange our own (self) righteousness for God's righteousness. In light of how the word *righteousness* is used many times in the Bible, we need God and the grace that comes through His Son, Jesus.

This righteousness from God comes through faith in Jesus Christ to all who believe.

Romans 3:22 NIV

Receiving this grace, or unmerited favor, will allow us to be put into the right position, and that is the position of righteousness or right standing with God through Jesus, just by believing and accepting this grace.

Be Skillful in the Word

This principle (the word of righteousness according to the righteousness of God) can be applied to many areas. Being skillful in your area of interest is important to your faith too. Is it your bent in life? Does it come natural to you? If so, have you given yourself to the field of studies about the area that you desire to go into? Do you know as much as you can about it? Do you have a passion for it? After you have studied it and you know that this is your purpose in life, would you do it if you did not get paid?

Yet, you may still be unskillful in the most important area. We can educate the mind but not the spirit. Remember, the spirit must be reborn, and once reborn, we must take another step by learning and placing importance in the Word of God. You could be the chief executive officer of a business or a schoolteacher or a business owner or be involved in some other field, but are you still unskilled in the Word of God? Do you leave this area only to the preachers?

You are skilled, talented in many areas (you may not believe this, but you are), because God created every person that way. But are you skilled in using the word of righteousness, which is completely and totally tied together in receiving the Word of God?

A person cannot hear the Word of God and be skillful in it if they only hear but don't do what they hear. When we hear, we do. You can't just hear it; you have to hear it *and use it*. You use it by applying it to your life in your thoughts, what you speak, and in your actions.

If you begin to hear the Word of God and use it, you will not be the same kind of person. You will become skillful in the Word, just like you have become skillful by studying other books related to your expertise. Add the Word of God to your life, and victory is bound to happen.

You see, your faith will no longer be located in your own smarts, or your own skills, but in the Word of God. You will be a powerhouse of faith, and faith is the victory that overcomes the world system or the difficulties of life—your faith in a higher power, the power of God working in you and through you; a supernatural power, the Word of God, working with the natural that's you—and there will be more physical things you will see as a result.

If you become skillful in the Word, wherever you presently are in life right now, there will only be "up" for you. You will propel yourself to a higher level. No more frustration because of stagnation; and you will be ready to be a teacher and tell others about this power (of God) that's available to them too.

Remember, Hebrews 5:12 says that we ought to be teachers by now, and teachers know more than the students.

I remember when I was going through broadcasting school (I went to a technical college at an early age). I applied myself for a year and a half to everything I could learn about broadcasting—radio first, and then television—and learned everything I could learn as a teenager and young adult.

By the time I was six months from graduating (because I was in high school at the same time), the school offered me a job at the technical college to be a teacher. So I went to work for them and taught broadcasting before I had graduated from high school, proof that being skillful in the things of God has nothing to do with your status in life, popularity, race, or gender.

You could say I passed the "milk stage," even though I was still young in age, and went into the teaching stage of this career.

Everyone who partakes only of **milk** *is unskilled in the word of righteousness for he is a babe, but solid food belongs to those who are of full age.*

Hebrews 5:13-14

What does this mean? When you use the Word of God regularly instead of using your emotions or how you feel, instead of using the opinion of others or what the economy is, you become skillful in using the Word of God. Now you have something that is powerful to use in every season of your life. There is no more need for you to whine, cry, and complain (like a baby does). By reason of use, the Word is your most skilled way of handling problems in life, and using it is how you grow up in the Lord.

When you use something over and over, it eventually becomes natural to do things that way. If you do not use your arm, for instance, you will not be able to use your arm for a period of time until your muscles get used to your using them again. In the same way, you must use the Word of God to see results; not just hear a good sermon, but use what you hear.

Whether you are 19 or 29 or 99, if you are not skilled in using the Word, then you need a bottle. By this time, you have teeth as big as mine, but you are sucking on a bottle. There is something wrong with that picture. The truth is, you will get in the habit of using what you make yourself get in the habit of using.

Drug addicts get used to drugs. They take them again and again simply because they are used to it. An alcoholic's body gets used to that alcohol. Smokers actually get used to smoke. People who eat a lot of sugar will go through sugar withdrawals when they try to stop eating sugar because their body is used to the amount of sugar they consume. If they stop eating that amount of sugar, they can go through flu-like symptoms for about three days. They feel as if they want to be in bed resting because they are going through sugar withdrawal.

So your body can get used to your doing something over and over again. It's the same with your spiritual life. You can get used to doing what is right and doing what works, if you practice what is taught in the Bible. But you have to make yourself use the right thing, even if you want to take a shortcut and use the wrong things to get ahead in life.

When the problems come up, don't take anything else as the source of your victory; you are skilled in the Word and have trained yourself to say, "I am going to use the Word of God. I'm going to find out what the Word says and apply it to my situation." You may have to get help from someone who is more skilled in the things of God, but help is available if you search it out. Every problem known to mankind can be solved, and actually every problem is already solved if we do it God's way.

Proverbs 16:25 NIV says, "There is a way that seems right to a man, but in the end it leads to death. Remember, death is not only physical death but also spiritual death, which means a separation from you and the truth. Jesus said, "I am the way, the truth, and the life" (John 14:6). In Him is the way (not a way, but the way) that will lead you into victory. In Him is the truth. Don't we want truth?

Most people are looking for truthful people, truthful pastors, truthful lawyers, truthful doctors, truthful teachers, truthful politicians—most human beings want truth to prevail. In God, you can find truth, and true life. You don't have to just exist, you can really live.

I like what the Bible said about King David, that "he died in a good old age, full of days and riches and honor" (1 Chron. 29:28). I believe David is not the only one who can experience this type of good life. He did not die weak, broke, or with dishonor, and we don't have to either.

If you know the story about his life, he was far from perfect. He committed adultery, and murder, but he repented to God with a true heart. He was sincere when he asked for forgiveness. He prayed and asked God to create in him a clean heart and renew in him a right spirit. (See Ps. 51:10.) Sometimes we try to move on in life, but we seem to be at a standstill. It's possible that there just might be a few unsolved issues that we must deal with first.

If we've wronged anyone or cheated anyone, I believe we need to go before God and ask for forgiveness and get our hearts right. Is it worth it to climb the corporate ladder and hurt everyone along the way as you climb? No, we must care about how we treat other people as we go forward in life so that when you reach the top, you have other people at the top with you.

I encourage you to say this out loud: *I will pursue God's written Word; that is how I am going to get victory in my personal life, my relationships, my emotions, and in seeing what I am seeing in my heart come to pass.* Practice being skillful in the Word of God, and you will find out how to treat other people and how to handle your success.

CHAPTER 9

Assessing Your Life

As soon as my birthday comes around, my wife starts asking me, "Well, Don, how do you feel about your life right now?" You see, on every birthday I take a look at my life and go through an assessment of it. I look at the accomplishments I made and the accomplishments I'm still working on. I assess my personal life, the ministry I have, my relationship with God, my financial areas—I take a survey over my entire life in all different kinds of ways. I look at where I am, and this is the time I begin to make some demands from myself.

I usually have met most of my goals right before my birthday because I know in my mind I'm going to ask myself, "Where are you," by that time. I really believe that you have to put a demand on yourself like that once in a while. This is called self-assessment, and it includes an evaluation of your abilities, actions, and attitudes. Before we look at several areas to assess regularly in your life that are vital to becoming a winner, I want to emphasize something.

There's nothing wrong with self-assessment as long as you understand that you are not out to please any human being—not even yourself. You should be doing what you believe God would have you to do. Success should not be measured alongside of someone else's life. You are not wise if you compare yourself with others, yet some people put that kind of stress on themselves of trying to live up to the Joneses.

We tend to live for other people and not what God put inside of us. If you are fulfilling your God-given purpose, then that is success. Let me take the pressure off you: Your life does not consist in the abundance of the things you can possess. Your life should consist of pleasing your Maker.

If God is pleased, that settles it. God said that He will give you the desires of your heart. I believe that you will receive those desires as you dedicate your life to Him. The truth is, He'll give you desires, and then He will give the ability to do them.

One way you'll know your God-given desires is that they just won't go away. This is where you will find contentment in life. Now, contentment is not mediocrity. Contentment is being thankful for what you have already—every bit of progress. Basically, I believe that a person who discovers their God-given desires is not a complainer. When you are a complainer, you may have to wander in the wilderness more often than you like. That's what happened to the children of Israel.

God gave them a vision for a better land, and once they were freed from bondage by a leader named Moses, who was sent by God to lead them to the land of promise, they got discontented and started to complain. Because they murmured, they went around in the wilderness in a circle for 40 years—and yet it was only a three-day journey.

Think about it: the Israelites went around in a circle, treading on the same ground for years and didn't know they were going in a circle. You would think that at some point they would have said,

"This looks like the same place I've been before." But no, they were complaining the whole time, and their complaints blinded them to their surroundings.

Complaining is actually a form of stress and depression, because people who complain are very unhappy people. They are stressed out about life and usually they are pessimistic about everything. This can cause depression and also fogginess in their mind, with the result of invisibility—they can't see where their life is going. That's why when driving in fog you need to put on special lights called fog lights so you can see better.

How can you assess where you've been if you do not know where you are going?

Does that describe you? Perhaps you have been walking in circles for too long and haven't realized it until now. Maybe you haven't realized that you have been in mediocrity for years. If so, you cannot just become another number. You cannot become just another working Joe. You must get yourself out of that because God did not have you become born again to live that way. I believe you are headed out of the wilderness, as you assess where you are and where you are headed.

Here are some more areas of self-assessment.

Expect Exponential Expectation

What are you expecting? Since God is working in your life, you can expect big. Remember, He will give you desires (in your heart), and then He will give you those desires (physically). What God will give you will be big. What else can the God who created the universe give someone? How can a big and awesome God give you a still or small vision? No, you should have exponential expectation for the next season in your life. You have done well, but it's time to move on and beyond what you can only think about.

"Now to Him who is able to do exceedingly abundantly above all that we ask or think, according to the power that works in us."

Ephesians 3:20

You are not designed to be mediocre. Do you know what the word means? It is neither very good nor very bad, just average. Does that sound exciting? Not really, especially when you know that God is able, not you. Now that's exciting news! It will definitely take the pressure off your shoulders to know that you can't do it anyhow, and it means that you should have fun in life!

God is not going to leave you high and dry. He will never leave you nor forsake you. (See Heb. 13:5.) Oh, I know that you feel that He has sometimes; but He hasn't. We just leave Him—His way of doing and being right. The problem is never with God, it's with us. He is a doing God, and He is able to do exceedingly abundantly above—He will go above, not below—what we will ask or even think. So it is to our advantage that we have big expectations to start with. God is not weak and He is not broke and He is not sick nor is He disabled. God fills in the entire gap.

I am not speaking unfavorably to disabled people; I'm letting you know that if you are physically disabled, with God you're not in the sense that He still will go above what you are expecting.

God is not partial, He shows no favoritism, and He is not prejudiced. So there is no excuse for failure. Some people will show favoritism, and some people unfortunately are prejudiced, but not God. He is an able, doing God who is waiting only for you to get the power working in you. What is this power that works in you?

It is the power to believe and the power to expect big things from a living God.

Knowing that God is not dead but fully alive is liberating. When you know the truth, the truth will set you free. When you believe and have faith in God, who is alive, then good and lasting things can happen for you. We are the only ones who disable an able God.

> *"Yes, again and again they tempted God, and limited the Holy One of Israel."*
>
> Psalm 78:41

The word *limited* here means "grieve"[3] and of course it does mean to set a boundary. This verse indicates that the Israelites set a boundary regarding God's power that they believed He couldn't pass. They had things they needed done that they felt He couldn't perform, and He didn't—because of their lack of faith in Him.

We can actually stop the hand of God, as it were, by our unbelief. The tradition, or the way we see things, can nullify the Word of God if we let it. Why limit an unlimited God? Since He created the universe, I believe He can handle whatever we ask of Him. We can grieve (limit) Him by not trusting in Him, so I encourage you to believe that He wants the best and has the best already laid for you. Just set your expectations high according to your faith (what you can believe) and He can surpass it every time. Remember, He is all-powerful, all-knowing, and He is everywhere—for God is God—and He will work in you and through you.

Sounds unbelievable, I know, but it is up to you to believe. You have believed other people and other things in life, so why not turn your attention to God and trust Him. Don't just try God, trust God. Remember, I will tell you only what has and is working for me and I know will work for you. Allow me to share one more thing for you to think about regarding expectations.

Ageing is inevitable if you continue to live longer on earth, and it is a known fact that people who retire and, in a sense stop expecting in life, soon die. It is said that a person lives on an average of about two years after retirement. So I want to get you past just thinking about retirement and try to get you to think about re-firement.

You need to get re-fired, not retired. You don't need to look at what year you will be going into the easy chair; you need to look at how long you are going to be out of that easy chair. You must get a different mentality about the things that God wants to do in your life.

Ageing should not be a death sentence. It should be looked at as just another season in life that you will go through. When I became a grandfather for the first time, initially I felt that I was old until I stopped myself and said, "I am not old; it's just another season in life."

I'm sure you have heard this, or maybe you have said this yourself about your children as they have gotten older, or maybe you said something like this to your oldest child: "You are starting to make me feel old." Don't say that. Moses confronted the Pharaoh of Egypt at the age of 80 years old. Can you picture Moses at 80 demanding Pharaoh to let the children of Israel go free? He told Pharaoh, "Let my people go!" Just imagine the energy, the strength, and the power that was in His words.

He didn't stop at the first, the second, the third, the fourth, the fifth, the six, the seventh, the eighth, the ninth, the tenth try, either. He didn't say that he was too old for this; he just kept being persistent because he had heard from God, and he had high expectations. All of his previous younger years were just preparation time.

You are not finished when you reach retirement age; you have more to give. In fact, as long as you have breath in your body and blood running through your veins, you still have something to accomplish on this earth. Expect big things and believe that they are coming to pass. Don't believe one minute and quit the next. You believe what the Word of God says.

Even when you are baking a cake, do you know that you can't keep opening the oven door to see if it's being baked? Some people keep closing the oven door, opening the door, and looking at the cake as if the oven is not going to work. The next time they open the oven door and close it, the cake falls completely flat because they didn't trust the process. They didn't trust that the oven was baking the cake without their help. That's what happens to those who have a lack of faith—their expectations fall flat.

Maybe you're in that group. You've kept opening the oven door and looking at the cake until it just said, "Leave me alone," and the cake just died out. God is able, but you have to learn how to use your faith, like baking a cake, trusting that it is working though it may take time. Opening that oven door too much is changing the temperature and the cake just says, "Forget it; that's it. I'm done," and it goes flat.

It sounds silly, but I'm sure you get the point, and that's what matters. God wants you to expect big, and if you do, then you will ask big and He will do His part. Along with your asking, I am not saying that you do nothing after that. No, now that you are trusting God to bring it to pass, He will tell you (in your heart and through the Word) every step that you need to make. There is work to be done, but at least now you know that you are not alone; you have supernatural help.

Casting Your Cares

When you are starting on any new venture, there will be times that you will be tempted to worry, and occasionally you may yield to that temptation. Think of it this way: When you worry, you are not in faith but in doubt, and doubt is a form of fear. The basis of doubt is rooted in fear and past experience. Worry, doubt, or fear will rob you of the very thing that you are setting your heart on.

I want to strongly emphasize that you must fight tooth and nail the temptation to worry. Yes, it is possible to live worry free. One way to fight worry is by casting the care, or you could say the concern, over to God. The load is too much for you to carry, so why not try what I'm about to tell you?

You have to learn how to cast your cares on somebody else. First Peter 5:6 says, "Humble yourselves under the mighty hand of God, that he may exalt you in due time." Once you start by faith and you believe by faith, there comes a time that the clock begins to tick. I believe this is a spiritual clock in our spirit that turns on when we start to walk by faith. This clock has a spiritual timer that starts ticking towards what is called *due time.*

Due time is the time that you will actually receive what you started believing for. One day the alarm is going to go off and you will have it. At that due time, every bit of what you are believing for will come to pass—but it's going to take some time to reach due time, and that's why we need faith.

Faith is what we use until the thing we believed for, over time, is received. Due time has arrived, but it started with casting your cares and believing God's promises.

First Peter 5 goes on to say in verse 7 that we are to cast all— not casting a few, or casting what you can, or casting everything but the big ones, or casting the little ones and keeping the big ones, but, casting *all* your care upon God—because He cares for you. I like to put it this way: Everything you care about you are to cast on Him. If you care about your children, you cast it on Him. If you care about your family, you cast it on Him.

You may be thinking right now, *Well, tell me, how do I cast it on Him?* I'm glad you asked! Before I answer that, let me give you an illustration of what it's like to carry your cares and how God can help you with them.

You can look at it in an agricultural term. As sheep grow with their wool and the wool gets heavy, they start waddling with those little legs. And after a period of time, if they walk into an indentation on the ground that turns them this way and that, they'll start wobbling until they roll upside down by mistake. With all that heavy wool on them, it causes them to be unbalanced to the point of rolling over. If they don't have a good shepherd around them, after a period of time, the little sheep will be upside down, or what is called *cast*. That sheep needs a shepherd, which is a human being who must be a good shepherd that watches over all the sheep.

Watching his flock even by night, the shepherd must be able to see when any sheep has turned cast, or upside down. They are so full of wool, they couldn't turn themselves over (right side up), even if they wanted to. So they need the shepherd to help them turn right side up. They are in a bad situation because the blood starts running from the little legs down into the chest cavity, and it will suffocate the sheep and kill them if they are not turned right side up in time.

This is a wonderful example of what you must do, and have the privilege of doing. You can cast your cares onto God as if you are upside down and ready to die. The shepherd has to physically lift that sheep up with all that wool on it and rub the four little legs to get the blood moving again. Then the little sheep starts going again, and soon it's as healthy as the other sheep in the sheepfold. God can lift you up too when you cast your cares on Him.

Some things need to die—maybe business deals or bad relationships—but let God determine that for you. If you cast these cares or any other cares onto Him, then you are taking your hands off the situation and you are saying to God, "Here, God, I trust You to work this out." He may speak to your heart and say, "Let the relationship die; it's over," or "Let the business die and start another one," or He may resurrect a relationship you thought was dead, or a business venture you thought was over. But unless He turns it back around and starts rubbing the little legs, you don't want it.

Knowing that God cares for you is important. If you really believe that He cares for you, you can trust Him with your very life. So how do you cast your cares upon Him? That's a good question, and one that is easy to answer. I will answer it by giving you something practical to do.

Take a piece of paper and write down everything that causes you concern. Write down your fears and the things you are worrying about. After you write these things down, pray and tell

God that you have written down everything that concerns you. Let Him know that you realize you cannot change these things and you are tired of worrying about them. Just be honest; He knows what is in your heart already, but you still have the need to express them to Him.

When you confess your faults to someone that you know cares (and we know God cares), you open the door for healing to take place in your life.

You were never created to carry burdens. Stress can open the door for sickness, and you don't want that. So express your heart to God, and after you have done this, throw the piece of paper in the wastebasket. Once you have thrown the paper away, use this as an act of your faith that it is over. You have cast your care unto God.

Now, don't go back and dig through the trash to retrieve that piece of paper. You may not physically do it, but if you start to worry again, then it is as if you reached your hand into the wastebasket and picked up the paper that you threw away. You just took your cares back from God. I admit that it will take self-control to not do this, but if you take your cares back, submit them again and again. One day as you learn to trust in God, you will be able to cast your care onto Him and finally leave them where they belong—in the care of a loving and caring God.

As you continue to hear the Word of God and read the Bible, you will develop a trustworthy friendship with God. You will know that He has only good things waiting for you. Like any true and lasting relationship, it takes time to develop. That's why it is so important to stay consistent—reading, praying, and hearing the good news of Jesus Christ. There is power in His name, and that is the power that is working in you.

Power in the Name

In assessing your life, maybe you realize that you didn't know the power in Jesus' name. Anytime you hear the name *Christ,* it's not Jesus' last name, just like Messiah (Jesus the Messiah) was not His last name—it's His description. The actual meaning of *Christ* is "anointed" or "the anointed,"[2] referring to power. So the name "Jesus Christ" or the description "Christ" is filled with power, and His name and faith in His name can make you well in every area of your life. To illustrate this, let's look at a certain man in the Bible who was lame.

Every day this lame man sat along the roadside near the temple begging for money, and the day that the apostles Peter and John walked by was no different. When the beggar saw them, he asked them for alms (money), but they knew that he needed to get well physically; then he could work and earn some money instead of begging for it.

Peter told the man that he did not have money to give him, but what Peter did have he would give to the man. What Peter and John had was the name of Jesus, and they knew the power that was in that name. So with that name Peter demanded that the lame man get up and walk, which he did.

People who witnessed the power of healing in the lame man marveled and thought that the power of Peter and John had made this man well, but Peter and John quickly corrected them.

By faith in the name of Jesus, this man whom you see and know was made strong. It is Jesus' name and the faith that comes through him that has given this complete healing to him, as you can all see.

Acts 3:16 NIV

The Bible also says that Jesus' name is above every name. (See Phil. 2:9.) Do you know why that is exciting? The name of Jesus Christ is above depression, cancer, or any other type of sickness or mental issues or debt or a broken heart—any name that is named—all because of Christ being the Anointed One.

The anointing is the power of God which removes burdens and destroys yokes. So anytime you talk about Christ, you are talking about burdens being removed from your shoulders and yokes being destroyed. What are these things? You may understand this as carrying a heavy load.

You were never designed or created to worry or be stressed out. God created man free from worry and free from stress. If He thought that it was good, He would have made sure that something in the creation was difficult so that Adam and Eve, the first man and woman that He made, would have some reason to worry or become stressful. No, everything was perfect—the surroundings and the work that God gave man to do. He told man to take care of the garden that He placed him in, but even that was easy to do.

After God created everything including mankind, He took a step back (I can imagine this), looked at all that He had done, and said, "This is very good." (See Gen. 1:31.) It took six days to complete His job and there was nothing else to add to or subtract from to His work. Because of everything being made very good, and mankind being made in God's image, He set aside the seventh day for rest. Rest is the vision God has for you—to live in a restful state in a restless world.

God knew that mankind could not have this rest outside of Him, so He spent time fellowshipping every day with Adam and Eve. But after that relationship was broken by sin, God immediately implemented the plan to redeem mankind back to Himself. We were actually created to worship God, and anything other than directing our worship to Him opens the door for a life of unrest. It was never meant for you to handle anything on your own, and now that we can have this broken relationship healed, we can have this supernatural power to work on our behalf.

The anointing is the supernatural power of God that will handle the things that concern you and remove them from your life—things that are too big for you to handle, too hard for you to take care of yourself. You do not, and I repeat *do not,* have to handle them on your own. You have help, but not just anyone's help; you have God's help, which is supernatural help. He will work every divine appointment needed for you, He will bring the people that He will give you favor with to help you. Yet it's not really a person helping you, it's God influencing that person to help you.

When the children of Israel needed help, they cried out to the living God, and God sent a man named Moses to deliver them from Egyptian bondage. But actually their cry was bigger than that, and eventually God sent His only begotten Son, Jesus Christ, to redeem us from the hand of the real enemy, Satan. He bought us back from Satan's pawnshop. Now when we become born again, we are in God's loving care once again.

Oh, what a restful place, to know that God cares for you!

Victory in Hard Places

God has provided you with His power to do all the things that are impossible for you to do. God will fight your battles for you, if you will allow Him. All you need to do is cast your cares and follow His plan; He'll take care of the rest. You must remember that what is impossible for you is possible for Him.

Are you starting to believe this? I hope so, because it is Bible-based truth. Here are some ways to cast your cares onto God; we've already mentioned the first two, but you must do every step. Are you ready to get carefree?

1. *Write down on paper everything that is in your heart that you are worried about.* Or just take one issue at a time (this is a good way to overcome negative habits you desire to break in your life too).

2. After you write down what you are worried about or the bad habit you have that you want to overcome, *pray by asking God in the name of Jesus to help you get the victory in these areas.*

   Remember, there is power in the name of Jesus.

3. *Whatever it is that you are concerned with, find a Scripture that relates to that area and start quoting that Scripture.* You can change your atmosphere of fear to faith. Look at this example. Say you are concerned about your children. Many parents find the passage in the Bible that says, "Great shall be the peace of your children" (Isa. 54:13), but that is only the second part of the verse. I'll explain this in the next step.

4. *Now you must obey what the passage of Scripture is telling you to do.* Usually, there is an act of obedience first in a particular verse that you must do. To have success you must read and commit to make confessions and then do the promise. In this verse the first part of it says, "All your children shall be taught by the Lord"; *then* it says, "And great shall be the peace your children." Teach your children about the goodness of God while they are young. If you messed up this opportunity, know that you can still make this wonderful promise your confession. Just ask God to forgive you and then begin to confess this verse over your children.

5. *Hear the Good News daily.* I like to put on a CD of a preacher teaching the Word of God (including my own CDs). Hearing the Word will inspire you but will also give you direction in your life. Expect God to talk to you in this way, and He will. I have had many people over the course of my years of preaching walk up to me and say that they received exactly what they needed from the message. I actually had counseling sessions cancelled because a person would get their questions solved in a church service.

There are so many wonderful promises in the Word concerning every area of life. Search for yourself and watch the power of God do wonders in you in the mighty name of Jesus, the Anointed One.

Now let's continue with our focus on the supernatural power available for you in God.

No Longer Yoked

Some people grew up around farms that had oxen which were occasionally yoked together. The yoke is a wooden bar or frame with two arched areas that fit over a pair of oxen's heads or necks and causes them to work together. Usually one of the oxen is big, but he will not plow as well on his own. He needs another ox to be with him. So the farmer yokes together a little ox with the big ox.

The little ox's neck is much smaller in the opening so that he can move his neck all over the place, but wherever the big ox goes that little one has to go along with him because he is bigger and they are yoked together.

That's how it is when people are yoked with Satan, who is the enemy to their faith. This is another important area to assess—are you yoked with God or with the enemy? Some things we cause to happen ourselves, but according to John 10:10, Satan comes to steal, kill, and destroy. He does that through evil forces and fallen angles (which are demons), led by him, who go to work against what is right. (See 2 Cor. 10:3.)

As a society, we have covered our eyes to these evil forces plaguing our nation and people way too long. I have found from reading the Bible that the evilness we experience in our nation is originating from an evil source. I believe there are evil forces, or spirits that also try to work against you and me, and they often work through some people. What evil people do comes from the heart, but the source is from the evil one.

It's a serious thing to play with the occult, the dark side of life. It's just as serious to live without God in your life because it leaves you wide open and defenseless to Satan's attacks. God said that He called us out of darkness, into His marvelous light, which means that there is a dark side, an evil force (Col. 1:13), and it can settle in the hearts of people to do evil things.

In Mark 7:20-23, Jesus said, "What comes out of a man, that defiles a man. For from within, out of the heart of men [and women], proceed evil thoughts, adulteries, fornications, murders, thefts, covetousness, wickedness, deceit, lewdness, an evil eye [envy], blasphemy, pride, foolishness. All these evil things come from within and defile a man [or woman]." Did you notice where evil comes from? According to this passage, it comes from the heart of people—but the origin of these things comes from Satan.

Remember, it's Satan who comes to steal, kill, and destroy; not God. We blame God far too much regarding bad things that happen. Why don't we put the blame where it belongs, on the enemy, Satan? I'm sure there are times when you know that you have done all you can in your power, and still everything seems to go wrong. Not in all cases, but I believe something has influenced many situations—Satan has been working against you.

Before you were born again, you were yoked up with the enemy (as is anyone without God), and wherever he wanted to take your life, you had to go. Wherever the demons (evil spirits that can work through other people or things) suggested going, that's where you ended up, and you were side by side with the enemy because you were yoked up with him. After you become born again that can still happen, if you don't know what God has given you to destroy Satan's yoke and win.

You do not have to be alarmed. You can have power over the work of the enemy if you are born again and submitted to God. We discussed becoming born again earlier; being submitted to

God simply means that you are submitted to the teachings of Jesus and His Word. In fact, the Book tells about this in James 4:7 AMP, "So be subject to God. Resist the devil [stand firm against him], and he will flee from you".

You stand firm against the devil by standing on (or holding onto) what is in the Bible. The Word of God is your weapon against Satan. We've already talked about the Word, but here's another important point: Stand firm on what God said about you, not anyone else, and don't forget that whatever is in your way, call it removed, in Jesus' name. *You* must do it; don't wait for anyone else, not even your pastor; he may not be available when you need this done. Remember, you have the victory in your mouth.

This may be an unpleasant thing for you to talk about, or think about, and I'm not encouraging you to make it your main focus. But learning how to fight unseen evil forces is imperative for every believer. When you take a stand against the enemy, don't be fearful, because once you turn your life over to God, Satan has no control or right to you any longer.

Maybe you never saw it like this: The negative force is rooted in Satan's camp, but once you are born again, you are in God's camp under His care and no longer yoked with what is bad. So, when I talk about Christ, I am talking about the burden-removing, yoke-destroying power—not to *break a yoke,* but to *destroy* it, because broken things can be fixed. That kind of power is available to you from God to stop the enemy, the big ox, from taking you places you don't want to go. Before, you just couldn't do anything about it; now you can.

At times Satan's evil forces will still try to work against you, but now they have no right to win. You have the power to get victory over these opposing troublemakers because you know that the power of God destroys the works of these unseen spirits, in the name of Jesus. So you can get the victory in hard places.

If you are just learning about this, you will see a miraculous change in your life as you take this control back. You thought it was just you, but it was a lesser power working against you to stop you or to discourage you long enough to make you want to quit. Thank God you didn't, yet you may know of some people who did. Our hearts go out to those who maybe didn't get this message in time, but you have, and you can tell others.

Know this: once you get Christ involved in your life, you get His power brought into your life—burden-removing, yoke-destroying power that enables you to win against the odds that are against you.

CHAPTER 10

Are You Dressed for Success?

Too many people have gone from one bad situation to another not realizing that they were fighting a spiritual battle, not a flesh one. We think it's that person standing in front of us who has caused us problems—it may be an abuser, or a person who is rejecting you because of your race, for instance—but it's not that person; it's the spirit behind that person making them act that way.

In the last chapter, we saw that evil words and actions come from the hearts of people, but the origin of evil things is Satan. The evil one and his forces are also known as the principalities, the powers, the rulers of the darkness of this age, the spiritual hosts of wickedness in the heavenly (supernatural) places. (See Eph. 6:12.) These demons are troublemakers, and they have made enough trouble for you already. How can you win against these evil forces?

You may have to do some things in the natural, like get away from someone who is physically or sexually abusing you, but there are spiritual actions you should take as well.

According to the Bible, you have weapons to use against the enemy, but your weapons are not carnal. They are "mighty through God to the pulling down of strong holds" (2 Cor. 10:4 KJV). I am going to show you in the rest of this chapter what your weapons are and teach you how to use each one to pull down those strongholds and stand against the evil plans of the devil.

> *Put on the whole armor of God, that you may be able to stand against the wiles of the devil. For we do not wrestle against flesh and blood, but against principalities, against powers, against the rulers of the darkness of this age, against spiritual hosts of wickedness in the heavenly places. Therefore take up the whole armor of God, that you may be able to withstand in the evil day, and having done all, to stand.*
>
> Ephesians 6:11-13

How do you stand against the devil, being effective and getting the supernatural power of God working on your behalf so you will win against all odds? We've already talked about the first way—you must imagine right. You must learn how to cast down negative imaginations and replace them with a mental picture of the life you want. Then start calling for that kind of life by saying it until it has manifested. Remember, don't let go of what you "see" in your heart for your life.

The second most important way to stand is to be dressed right! I'm not talking about physical clothing, but about the spiritual armor you have available, given by God. The reason you need armor on is that often you will be engaged in active spiritual battle with the enemy; the armor of God, which works in a supernatural way, works against the invisible opposing evil forces that will try to stop you from winning.

Jesus is the best example of someone who knew how to wear the armor and use it against the devil. When Jesus was tempted by him in the wilderness, the Bible says that finally Satan ended the attack and "retreated temporarily, lying in wait for another opportunity" (Luke 4:13 MSG).

Matthew Henry explains this, saying, "[Satan] then quitted the field: he departed from [Jesus]. He saw it was to no purpose to attack [Jesus]; [Jesus] had nothing in him for [Satan's] fiery darts to fasten upon; [Jesus] had no blind side, no weak or unguarded part in His wall, and therefore Satan gave up the cause. Yet he continued his malice against [Jesus], and departed with a resolution to attack Him again [later on]."[1]

You can see the truth here that Satan's attacks will come, but the power of God will work through you as you stay dressed for war. In the physical world, armor is used as a protective covering worn to protect the body against weapons. The same is true spiritually speaking. You need protection against Satan 24 hours a day, 7 days a week. So once you decide to put on this armor, don't take it off, no matter what your circumstances may be!

We're going to look at the whole armor of God next, piece by piece, because when you know how to use it, it will protect you and defend you as you fight to win.

Armor #1: Truth

Stand therefore, having girded your waist with truth.

Ephesians 6:14

The question has often been asked, "What is truth?" *Truth* is unmovable and unshaken. It is lasting and solid as a rock. *Truth* is honesty, loyalty, always giving and always forgiving.

Truth can be depended upon, never faltering; never leaving and never forsaking, even under the worst conditions. You can count on truth; it holds everything together in your life. *Truth* is never ending, you can come back to it in a thousand years or so and it will still be the truth—and truth is personified in the person of Jesus.

Jesus is *the* Way, not *a* way; He is *the* Truth, not *a* truth; and He is *the* Life, not a life. (See John 14:6.) People say, "Get a life," but I say, "Get *the* Life." When you put on truth as your armor, you put on Christ—and when you put on Christ, you put on power. (Rom. 13:12; Gal. 3:27.) You are no longer fighting on your own; you have supernatural strength in the boxing ring of life. His truth is a force that will lead and guide you through the darkest hours you face.

I like the poem that was written many years ago called *Footprints in the Sand*. Some say the author was a woman named Mary Stevenson. In this poem the author asked Jesus why she only saw one set of footprints during the hardest times in her life. The reply is awesome: Those were the times Jesus carried her, which meant that the only set of footprints belonged to Jesus. That is something I can personally say I have experienced.

In some of my darkness hours, when I thought that I was dealing with the challenges of life by myself, and my wife could not even help me, it was then I knew personally, after much prayer and meditation, that I had help. I could not see God, but I knew my Helper was with me.

The wisest and wealthiest man who ever lived, King Solomon, told us that we are to "buy the truth, and sell it not" (Prov. 23:23 KJV). Of course, you cannot physically buy truth, but this verse means that it is so valuable. When life gets tough, you may want to take a shortcut, even though in your heart you know that the choice is a dishonest attempt to satisfy your desire. Don't do it! Don't sell out! Stay a person of truth, by knowing *the* Truth.

God's way is *the* truth. Seek His way through the principles in the Bible. You can rely on what works because His words are pure, "like silver tried in a furnace of earth, purified seven times" (Ps. 12:6). Here are some other Bible passages regarding truth.

"My mouth will speak truth; wickedness is an abomination to my lips."

Proverbs 8:7

This is a daily choice.

"Truth stands the test of time; lies are soon exposed."

Proverbs 12:19 TLB

Why bring shame to you and your family?

"If a king is kind, honest and fair, his kingdom stands secure."

Proverbs 20:28 TLB

Truth is a sure way to guarantee your success in every area of your life.

"You shall know the truth, and the truth shall make you free."

John 8:32

Do you want to be free financially, spiritually, socially—in every area? Get *the* Truth regarding the matter, and you will make yourself free. Decide today to put truth on and never take it off. Be upfront about situations; don't run from your obligations. You will receive favor, and God will be with you.

Armor #2: The Breastplate of Righteousness

Stand therefore,...having put on the breastplate of righteousness.

Ephesians 6:14

The breastplate is a cover to protect the chest, which is where your physical heart is located. It represents your character and your integrity—both elements of righteousness. Albert Barnes in his Bible commentary says, "The idea here may be that the integrity of life, and righteousness of character, is as necessary to defend us from the assaults of Satan, as the coat of mail [or the breastplate] was to preserve the heart from the arrows of an enemy."[2]

People sometimes think that they can live a wild, uncontrolled life and reap a peaceful harvest. When we don't do right, especially when we know to do right, we deceive ourselves.

I'm sure you're familiar by now with the Bible's message we discussed earlier of whatever a person sows, that is what they will reap. If someone sows to their sinful nature what is bad, they will reap destruction; but if a person sows what is good, they will reap good. For example, if you sow kindness, you'll reap kindness; if you sow a smile, you will reap a smile. The principle holds true to any area—money, love, forgiveness, and on and on the list can continue. It's the nature of a seed. It's called seedtime and harvest. Whatever you sow you reap.

It does matter if we live a good life above reproach, so we must work at our character daily. Due to the fact that every day we have the same choice to make, we must decide, *Will I choose what is right or wrong in my affairs?* But the armor of God is a physical description with a spiritual meaning as well and, therefore, it also represents the work that was done by God through His Son Jesus.

> *God made him who had no sin to be sin for us, so that in him we might become the righteousness of God.*
>
> 2 Corinthians 5:21 NIV

Another way that this has been said is that God's goodness was poured into us. That means our righteousness (being free from guilt or sin) is of Him. (See Isa. 54:17.) With this knowledge you should realize that as you are standing to win, you may have "missed the mark" at some point, you may have fallen short, and now you have a stain on your character. Yet that is not a sign that you are finished and so you throw in the towel, go home, and put your head under the covers. You are not out of the race.

No, it's time for you to pick yourself up, dust yourself off (asking God for forgiveness, and if you wronged someone, making it right and never returning to that wrong again), and move on from where you have left off, or start over if you have to. But never quit! Make your setback a comeback, but make a decision to come back stronger, fighting every negative imagination that you are not worthy or that you are not good enough.

Since you are in a faith fight (1 Tim. 6:12), only fight to win—and if you are going to win, win big! You are not all washed out. That's a lie of the enemy. You can never be perfect, none of us are; but God doesn't wipe you off the planet. He promised He would not send another flood to wipe out mankind again. (See Gen. 8:21–22.) You have the forgiveness that comes from God. People may not forget and forgive, but God has a wonderful ability to forget and forgive, and He has given us the ability to forget those things that need to be left in the past.

You must master the forgetful part, and you can. At least you can forget the pain of the past, like a woman will forget the pain of childbirth. This is the thought you must possess: *I am still not all I should be, but I am bringing all my energies to bear on this one thing:* "Forgetting the past and looking forward to what lies ahead,

I strain to reach the end of the race and receive the prize" (Phil. 3:13 TLB).

God will help you to forget if you allow Him to. Just by asking Him to help you forget the things that hurt you and the mistakes you have made, He will come in to do His part. But you must do your part by first making a decision to let go of the past and continue to run your race and not give up.

It's not hard to live this life if you are determined to do it God's way. What are you determined to do—stop or finish? You're not racing against any other person; you're on your own track, so you can go at your own pace. Some people may try to race against you, but you must stay focused on your goal. Don't take your eyes off your prize. Besides, if someone is trying to compete against you, doesn't that say that you have something they see and they like?

Here are some simple things you can do to put on the breast-plate of righteousness and live God's way—the way of a winner:

1. Have integrity.

2. If you do wrong, be quick to ask for forgiveness.

3. If someone has wronged you, be quick to show mercy.

4. Determine you will not quit.

5. Don't compete.

6. Sow good wherever you go, whatever you do.

7. Do things that will make others happy, and soon you will reap the same.

Armor #3: Peace

Stand therefore, having shod your feet with the preparation of the gospel of peace.

Ephesians 6:14-15

The word *shod* here just means to put on shoes, which implies readiness. As the Roman soldiers' feet in biblical times were shod with hard, nail or iron spike-studded shoes, and they were ready for battle, we too must be ready or prepared for spiritual battle with the gospel of peace.

Peace is another powerful force, so to have our feet shod with the gospel of peace means that peace helps us to be prepared to meet the enemy's attacks. With the focus in this verse being on peace, true peace comes from knowing God (or having a relationship with Him) and trusting Him through the Scriptures (the Word of God). Yet many people miss finding this real peace because they look for it in other places.

Every human being is born into this world with a void. Men and women, boys and girls, have tried to fill that void with everything instead of God. I did that myself. I tried other things that would satisfy what only God could ultimately do. Fame in the radio broadcasting industry did not do it for me. People wanting my autograph and calling my name did not do it for me. The truth is, after the stage lights went off and I went home, I was miserable and lonely. When I finally decided to place my life in the hands of God, that is when true life began.

Peace is not dependent on circumstances; it depends on a relationship, and that relationship starts with God. He is the only One who can keep you in perfect peace as you seek Him for strength.

He will keep in perfect peace all those who trust in him, whose thoughts turn often to the Lord!

Isaiah 26:3 TLB

Notice that the key here is turning your thoughts or fixing your mind on God. A good way to keep your mind on Him is by reading the Bible and praying daily. Let's look at some other Bible verses regarding peace.

[God] has redeemed my soul in peace from the battle that was against me.

Psalm 55:18

As we have seen, your soul is made up of your mind, will, and emotions. Even though you may have gone through the worst battle in your life, or you're in the worst battle of your life right now, just know that God can redeem your mind, your will, and your emotions—He can restore and give back to you the peace that belongs to you. He can comfort your soul. He can settle your mind. He can heal your brokenness (your emotions). He can do this by the comfort of the Scriptures.

Whatever things were written before were written for our learning, that we through the patience and comfort of the Scriptures might have hope.

Romans 15:4

Great peace have those who love Your law, and nothing causes them to stumble.

Psalm 119:165

Your peace is in the comfort of the words written in the Bible. Great peace is waiting for you there, the peace that is not obtainable in the world that you live in. In the middle of chaos, you can have peace by setting your mind on the words of Christ. Be determined to find this comfort in His words. It's that type of peace that will take you through hard times.

Peace I leave you; my peace I give you. I do not give to you as the world gives. Do not let your hearts be troubled and do not be afraid.

John 14:27 NIV

Therefore let us pursue the things which make for peace and the things by which one may edify another.

Romans 14:19

To *pursue* is to go after or chase after. That is the mindset we should have—to go after peace, not confusion or disharmony. Pursue the things that will bring unity and a peaceful situation with the understanding that you must work at this because some people just don't know peace.

My soul has dwelt too long with one who hates peace. I am for peace; but when I speak, they are for war.

Psalm 120:6,7

As this relates to our relationship with others, it's an unpleasant and sobering thought to admit that there are some people who are not for peace but only war. Do we not experience this in our own nation and surrounding nations? What should we do? Matthew 5:9 says, "Blessed are the peacemakers." In other words, try to live at peace with all people, if it's in your power to do so, for then you will be blessed—and that's true success.

Armor #4: The Shield of Faith

"Above all, [take] the shield of faith with which you will be able to quench all the fiery darts of the wicked one."

Ephesians 6:16

The shield of faith is a defensive weapon and was used to put out the fiery darts of enemies. Roman soldiers would use a fireproof shield to protect themselves from these flaming arrows. The shield could be turned in every direction so that no matter the direction of the fiery darts, the soldiers were able to put them out.

Notice in this verse that they are not just called darts, but fiery darts meant to do the most damage possible if the soldier was not skilled in using his shield. How does this relate to you? No matter what type of assault is used against you by any unseen evil force, you have available to you faith—total trust and confidence in God, His love, faithfulness, and power; and reliance on His Word and help.

I like the way John Darby describes this in his Bible commentary: "The work of the Spirit in us is to inspire this confidence. When it exists, all the attacks of the enemy, who seeks to make us believe that the goodness of God is not so sure—all his efforts to destroy or to weaken in our hearts this confidence in God and to hide Him from us, prove fruitless. His arrows fall to the ground without reaching us."[3]

The fact is, your faith causes God himself to be your shield.

[God] is a shield to those who put their trust in Him.

Proverbs 30:5

God's Word helps build our faith, so in that sense, it is a component of the shield of faith. We've already seen that the words written in the Bible are not just dead words but words that are very much alive. They are words that are Spirit, and they are life. (See John 6:63.) When spoken with faith, God's words will be your protector. Let me give you an example.

One of my favorite verses in the Bible, which I have taught thousands of people to use every waking day, is Isaiah 54:17 AMP. It says, "But no weapon that is formed against you shall prosper, and every tongue that shall rise against you in judgment you shall show to be in the wrong. This [peace, righteousness, security, triumph over opposition] is the heritage of the servants of the Lord [those in whom the ideal Servant of the Lord is reproduced]; this is the righteousness or the vindication which they obtain from Me [this is that which I impart to them as their justification], says the Lord".

I encourage you to declare this every morning, but you can make it simple by just saying, "No weapon formed against me shall prosper, and every tongue that rises against me in judgment, I condemn." What you are doing is putting out every fiery dart that was formed against you before you even leave the house.

Use the shield of faith by using the Word of God. (Remember, you use it by applying it to your life in your thoughts and in the words you speak.) It will put out not some, but all the fiery darts of the wicked one and stop him from making progress or succeeding against you.[4] Whatever he can come up with, you have the solution to win.

Armor #5: The Helmet of Salvation

Put on salvation as your helmet.

Ephesians 6:17 NLT

Naturally a helmet is used to cover the head for protection, so this piece of armor is just as vitally important as the rest. Why is it called the helmet of salvation? The word *helmet* once again refers to protection. The word *salvation* refers to many areas: having hope for what can occur now on earth in your life; the salvation you can experience while on earth, and hope for the future salvation that you have in heaven. *Salvation* is also being rescued from danger and sin; it is health, wholeness, and soundness.

God is your deliverer, He is your defender, and He is your sure reward. David said this in the book of Psalms, "Bless the Lord who is my immovable Rock. He gives me strength and skill in battle" (Ps. 144:1 TLB). David personally knew the God of his salvation. He was sure of the victory that he would be able to gain because David believed that he would not have to fight alone.

When David fought Goliath, David depended on the strength of his God. (See 1 Sam. 17.) Take note of Goliath's armor: a bronze helmet (most troops had only leather helmets); a coat of mail (the weight of the coat was five thousand shekels of bronze, which was about 125 pounds); bronze armor on his legs; a bronze javelin, which was designed for hurling; a spear and the spearhead (made of iron and weighing six hundred shekels, which was about 17 pounds); and his armor bearer walking before him with a huge shield.

Saul, who was king at the time, looked at the giant and then looked at David and tried to convince David that there was no way he would be able to fight Goliath. But David was fearless because he had seen God come through for him many times before, and David spoke to Saul of his many past victories.

Saul reluctantly allowed David to go into battle, but before he sent him off, Saul gave David his personal armor to put on. When David tried the armor on, it did not fit correctly for David was just a youth. David mentioned to Saul that Saul's armor was too big and that he could hardly walk with it on, and David chose not to use it.

After taking off Saul's armor, David picked up five smooth stones from a stream and put them in his shepherd's bag, and armed only with his shepherd's staff and sling, he approached his enemy. Goliath was all decked out ready for battle; his physical armor was the best at that time, and David had only a few stones, a staff, and a sling.

In the natural, if you had been there, you probably would have seen and believed that Goliath would win this fight. The reason is the fact that we are so prone to see only with our physical sight, not through our spiritual sight, which is supernatural. David had a few physical items that could not compare with his enemy's armor, but David was dressed with the armor of God, and he said to Goliath, "You come to me with a sword, with a spear, and with a javelin. But I come to you in the name of the Lord of hosts, the God of the armies of Israel, whom you have defied" (v. 45).

Notice that David did not say, "I come to you with a slingshot," because he knew that it wasn't going to win him this battle. David knew that only God could win this battle for him, and he expected to win—he knew that he would see the salvation of the Lord. In fact, David could have said the same thing that Moses said many years earlier when Moses faced an impossible situation: "Stand still, and see the salvation of the Lord" (Ex. 14:13).

David trusted God, not in the things he had to fight with, which wasn't much; but he knew that with God all things are possible. David was with God and God was with David, and David saw the Lord's salvation in his situation—he defeated Goliath with only one stone flung from his slingshot. (See 1 Sam. 17:49).

God will take the little you have, and if you give Him just a little to start with and trust Him, He will add to it and it will become much. What is in your hands that you think is insufficient? Use it, and then stand still and see the salvation of the Lord in your life.

Armor #6: The Sword of the Spirit

Take…the sword of the Spirit, which is the word of God.

Ephesians 6:17

The sword of the Spirit is the only offensive weapon in this armor, and as this verse says, it is the Word of God. But it is not necessarily the Bible as a whole; to use this sword you must start to speak a specific word from the Bible for your particular situation.

According to Adam Clarke's Bible commentary, "An ability to quote this on proper occasions, and especially in times of temptation and trial, has a wonderful tendency to cut in pieces the snares of the adversary."[5] That's why it is imperative for you to understand how the Word works in connection with the armor of God in order for you to win in life; otherwise, you will be defeated.

Defeat should not be in your vocabulary any longer. So I am going to explain the workings of the sword of the Spirit by using a few examples which I believe will be helpful for you. Remember, I will tell you only what works.

God's Word covers every area of life. That is one of the reasons why it is to your advantage to read the Bible daily. The Bible is not a good novel, full of interesting stories. Many times the true stories of David and Goliath and the wonderful birth of Jesus, who was born in a manger, are just thought of as a children's bedtime story.

In far too many cases, we have reduced these wonderful truths down to fairy tales, yet these are powerful truths from which we can learn important principles to live by.

In the midst of these principles are words inspired by the Spirit of God that should be used as a weapon against every evil force. It's like having a two-edged sword proceed from your mouth, which is actually what the writer of Hebrews compares the Word to. (See Hebrews 4:12.) Sounds strange, but when you put the Word of God in your mouth and speak it over your situation, it will go to work for you because the Word is alive and full of power.

When you speak the power-filled words of the Bible every day, you are speaking life into your life and your affairs. By doing this, you are inviting God's angels on the scene to help you. We talked about that earlier, but it is so important that I want to reemphasize it here.

> Bless the Lord, you His angels, who excel in strength, who do His word, heeding the voice of His word.
>
> Psalm 103:20

Remember, these angels are waiting for you to speak God's words from your mouth, because when you do, God will send them to work for you. To them, it is as if God himself is saying the words. They are waiting to be employed on your behalf.

Whatever your need is, there is a word for you from the Word of God. You must diligently search in the Bible as for gold, because these are nuggets hidden in its pages; ask God to reveal them to you.

What reliable word do you need? It is in the Bible, regardless of whether you need health, wealth, wisdom for a business transaction, directions for your children, freedom from worry, or something else—find God's Word on the matter, and make the positive confession of your faith. Here are a couple of positive confessions you can make over your life, but don't limit your confession to these only. Read the Book and find your own.

If you need health, 1 Peter 2:24 says, "Himself [Jesus] bore our sins in His own body on the tree, that we, having died to sins, might live for righteousness—by whose stripes you were healed." *Your confession would be:* "By Jesus' stripes I am healed."

You should continue to do what the doctor is telling you to do, of course, but you should also continue to make this your confession, "I believe I'm healed" (another way you can say it), every day until you receive the manifestation of your healing. When that happens, be sure to go back to your doctor so he or she can check you and verify that nothing is wrong with you.

If you need wealth, Deuteronomy 8:18 says, "You shall remember the Lord your God, for it is He who gives you power to get wealth, that He may establish His covenant which He swore to your fathers, as it is this day." *Your confession would be:* "God has given me the power to get wealth; therefore, I believe I am a wealthy person."

True success is not just acquiring material wealth, though, and many well-known people can tell you that; it's deeper than what any human being can see. Outside of God, true happiness can't be found—it's not found in your wallet, in your fame, in your cars, or in yourself. I believe it is found only in God. Then you can truly say, "He has given me richly all things to enjoy" (1 Tim. 6:17).

Remember, death and life are in the power of the tongue. You will live a victorious life when you speak the Word of God and a defeated life if you don't.

Armor #7: Praying Always

[Pray] always with all prayer and supplication in the Spirit.

Ephesians 6:18

You may say that prayer is not a piece of the armor, but don't forget that you are not in a physical war, you are in a spiritual war, and prayer is the most valuable weapon you can use. That is why I believe in this verse it tells us to pray always, *after* we are fully dressed in the armor of God.

Albert Barnes notes in his Bible commentary, "No matter how complete the armor; no matter how skilled we may be in the science of war; no matter how courageous we may be, we may be certain that without prayer we shall be defeated. God alone can give the victory; and when the Christian soldier goes forth armed completely for the spiritual conflict, if he looks to God by prayer, he may be sure of a triumph."[6]

Can you see how indispensable prayer is for us? So even though I have already covered the area of prayer, there are a few points I want to mention in this much-needed part of your life.

The apostle Paul says in this verse that we are to pray always, so prayer should be done on a continual basis. This is something that can be done while washing dishes, washing the car, driving down the street, or doing any number of things throughout the day, besides praying during the quiet time you set aside in a designated area to commune with God.

Prayer is twofold. When you pray you believe you receive, so that type of prayer is asking and receiving (which as we saw is called the prayer of petition or prayer of supplication). According to the Word, the results of prayer, or the manifestation of what you are believing for, will take place, but it may take some time. So faith and patience (or endurance) are needed in order for you to receive the goods.

Confidence is also needed when you pray, which will help you to endure until the manifestation comes. When I say that, I mean confidence should never be in your own ability but in the fact that God is able to do for you what you have asked of Him.

Now this is the confidence that we have in Him, that if we ask anything according to His will, He hears us. And if we know that He hears us, whatever we ask, we know that we have the petitions that we have asked of Him.

1 John 5:14-15

Your trust is in God. That is where your confidence should be and that is where it should stay. Sometimes it may seem like it is not working, but it is. Remember, tough situations will not last, but tough people will, if they trust the One who can do beyond what they can ask or think. (See Eph. 3:20.)

I am reminded of the story about the apostle Peter walking on the water. The Bible tells how the wind was contrary, and it was causing the boat that the disciples were in to be tossed by the waves. (See Matt. 14:24.) Here the disciples were in the middle of the sea, and now they are dealing with a problem. What is opposing you in your life? That is exactly what the word *contrary* means.

The wind was opposing the disciples, wreckage of the ship would have soon been unavoidable, and maybe they would have even lost their lives if Jesus hadn't stopped by (walking on water to get there). But Jesus started toward the boat, walking on the water, and when the disciples saw Him, they were afraid.

At first the disciples didn't know if it was Jesus or a ghost. Peter, being the bold one out of the group, wanted to know if it was the Lord, so he asked Jesus to allow him to come out and walk on the water to meet Him. Jesus gave Peter permission by saying one word, "Come." So Peter stepped out of the boat and walked on the water.

That is where you may be in your life right now—out of the boat, doing the impossible. Things may have been going just the way you had planned, and then, lo and behold, the wind became contrary in your life. Maybe your spouse walked out on you, or your business lost a big contract, and or something else happened that was contrary to your plans. In other words, the wind became boisterous. What are you going to do?

That is what happened to Peter. The wind started to rage, and instead of keeping his eyes on Jesus, Peter started to look at the wind: "But when he saw that the wind was boisterous, he [Peter] was afraid; and beginning to sink he cried out, saying, 'Lord, save me'" (Matt. 14:30). Peter was doing so well until he lost sight of the One who is able to do exceeding, abundantly, above all that you can ask or think. He stopped putting his trust in God and started to sink, until he cried out to Jesus to save him. Peter, in a sense, said a three-word prayer, "Lord, save me!" and the Bible says that immediately he received Jesus' help.

Have you stopped trusting God? If so, become like Peter—cry out to God; He will not turn His back on you. You can have confidence in the truth that if you ask anything according to God's will, He hears you. (Remember, God's will is His Word.)

Another way to look at it is that the promises in the Bible, which are only good, are yours. So you can rest assured that every good and perfect (complete) gift comes to us from God. (See James 1:17.) It's really that easy, but you must follow God's plan for your life.

To me the Bible is just like a recipe book for your life. All you have to do is follow the recipe and you will get the results you want. Whatever God does for you will not be half-baked. So, if God said you could have something, then you can have it. I know from personal experience—remember the building I wanted to buy? I thought everything was over when it was sold out from under me, but God had something new and a hundred times better for me.

When you trust God and have confidence in Him, He will bring you through the "storms" in your life. God hears you. You should know this. His "cell phone" never shuts off, His bill is paid for in advance. Day or night God is waiting for you. You're not really waiting on God, He is waiting on you to get in touch with Him. The good news is, He hears and understands you.

Have you ever told someone, "You just don't understand"? I have. In reality, no one—not even psychologists, counselors, doctors, teachers, mothers or fathers, sisters and brothers, ministers, and people in general—can fully understand some of the deepest thoughts of your heart. Only God can. He is waiting to hear from you and respond to your prayer.

This is your confidence and comfort—He hears and He will respond. Just be patient and believe at all times. Your change of season is soon approaching. Wait for it and you will not be disappointed, for God will never disappoint you!

CHAPTER 11

Living the Life of a Winner

The future for you is bright in God. That is what His Word says in many Scriptures. As you read through the Bible, you will find that it is not ungodly to know the future; it is ungodly to use ungodly means to divine the future events. The Holy Spirit is here to help us know our future victories by placing dreams and desires in us and flooding "[our] hearts with light so that [we] can see something of the future he has called [us] to…" (Eph. 1:18 TLB).

I like the Message Bible translation of this verse, which says that the Lord makes "you intelligent and discerning in knowing him personally, your eyes focused and clear, so that you can see exactly what it is he is calling you to do." You see, it does matter that God is in your life to help you to win.

In the Bible Joseph was a young man who became a winner against all odds because of his close relationship with God. This story is a great example of what God can do with you as you apply the principles in this book to your life. God had given Joseph the ability to operate in visions and dreams; his winning was not by chance or happenstance. It was spiritually predictable and forecasted by God's word to him, which made it a guarantee.

Joseph had a dream twice of being a winning leader and ruler of people in a great way, including with his own family. The problem was that he shared that dream with his unbelieving brothers. Now, you would think that everyone would love a winner, but many people make the mistake of telling their vision or plan of becoming a winner to those who do not desire to see them succeed in life. That's what Joseph did, with disastrous results.

Joseph's dream became a point of contention with his brothers and a brunt of many jokes against him. They called him "that dreamer" when he would come around them, and they disrespected and despised him and constantly talked against him. Their hatred of him because of his dream and his apparent favor with their father became so strong that they plotted to kill him to get rid of him. It was only the pleading of two of his brothers, Ruben and Judah, that caused them to sell him into slavery instead.

Joseph ended up in Egypt as a slave to one of Pharaoh's right-hand men, Potiphar, who was an officer and captain of the guards. (See Gen. 39:1.) As young Joseph was doing his appointed job well in the household of Potiphar, the Bible says that God was with him and caused everything that Joseph touched to prosper. (vv. 2-3.) He eventually won, through the means of God's favor, the position of manager of Potiphar's household.

This man with godly principles for winning in life, though he was hated by his own brothers and thrown into a pit to die, then later sold into slavery, ended up being sold to one of the king of Egypt's highest rulers, who placed Joseph as the manager of his household.

Can you imagine being left for dead in a pit, then taken out to be sold into slavery, and then having God orchestrate your destiny into the winning position of manager of the household of one of the most powerful men in the known world? That is what I call winning against all odds, wouldn't you? It is the kind of winning I am talking to you about getting used to seeing happen in your own life if you'll follow what I am saying to you in this book. Remember, I will tell you only what works.

While Joseph was doing an excellent job as the steward of Potiphar's entire household, Potiphar's wife saw the victory on Joseph's life, and how young, handsome, and successful he was. In other words, she could see that he was a winner.

Did you know you can see that on people? I believe people will start to see that on you more and more as you begin to apply these simple principles of winning that I'm sharing with you to your own life.

After a period of time, Potiphar's wife became very bold in her desire to commit adultery with Joseph. In spite of her advances, Joseph knew who he was and how he got there—and he refused to give in to her constant attempts to seduce him. Let's stop for a moment and think about this. Joseph not only knew he was big man on campus, but he knew that it had happened by following God's promises.

Some believers try to use God to get to the place of winning, only to forget how they got there once they begin to enjoy the victory. Whether it is winning financially in life, or in their long awaited business, career, political, sports, or relationship victory, time and time again people seem to make the same mistake that God's chosen people in the Bible (Israel) made. When they move into the new house, get the new job, the wealth, the fame, the recognition, the education, the power and position, the healing, or victory in some other way, they forget that it was God who gave them the avenue to win in life.

Joseph did not forget, and he did not celebrate his winning with smug confidence. He did not think to himself as many people do, *Now that I am a winner I can do no wrong. I am a winner, so it does not matter now how I live my life or who I live it with.* I believe that winners have a responsibility to God, whether they know Him or not.

Always remember that whatever you are winning in, you are ultimately using God's borrowed materials to have your victory. When victorious people neglect God, that is the cause for the emptiness that is left in their hearts—and they end up trying to fill that emptiness with other things in a wrong way.

Even if your biggest victory was being able to sit up in that hospital bed and feed yourself today, after a devastating physical attack or accident afflicted you to the point of not being as operable as you were just a few days ago—please know that it is God who gives each of us the ability to do what we are able to do, including win in life. We would be better off if we would thank God for the strength to do what we couldn't do before. That too is winning against all odds.

The Life of a Winner

Now Joseph was well-built and handsome, and after a while his master's wife took notice of Joseph and said, "Come to bed with me!" But he refused.

Genesis 39:6-8 NIV

Potiphar's wife had no right to demand that Joseph have a sexual encounter with her, especially to the point of pulling on his clothes and tearing off his tunic. As you can see from this passage, Joseph didn't give in to her demands. We can learn a number of things from this true story about the life of this winner, Joseph.

First of all, winners are attractive; the spirit of the winner attracts people. That is why some of us consistently want to know the inside story about famous people. What we may not realize is that many successful men and women have fallen into the trap of celebrating victory with the wrong people—and jeopardized their success.

Actually, the whole process on how to celebrate has been well-placed in our society through the media—with beer in hand, with wine being poured, with drunken parties, illicit sexual relationships—all being portrayed as the image of a real celebration for real winners. I am not saying you are not to enjoy celebrating the winning events in life, but you should put some care into the celebration in a couple of areas.

1. *Know who has a right to celebrate your success with you.* Certainly God did not give Joseph his position and cause him to "climb the corporate ladder" to have an affair with the boss's wife! That is not the proper way to celebrate your position, success, or persona either. Too often winners have allowed their victory celebrations to turn into a collection of memories of regrets that they wish they could forget. If we are not careful, we will fall into a life of winning only to consistently lose that win in the "after-work" celebrations.

Celebrating with the right people is important to remember also. Hard work to win can bring great rewards that are worth celebrating when the work is complete, but those who have learned how to win have to learn how to celebrate their winning.

2. *What form of celebration will you allow yourself to have? Will you celebrate with alcohol, drugs, food, sex, partying, or with prayer and quietness?* Too many tragedies happen when celebrations don't have parameters—becoming an alcoholic or a (prescription or illegal) drug abuser can begin with this kind of celebration. Because of the stress at work, for example, drinking or drug habits that began with a victory celebration can develop over the years to dull the effects of a hard day at the office or in the field.

I am not saying we should not have a good time, but I'm sure you know of celebrations that have turned to times of regret—serious or fatal drunk driving accidents or sexual promiscuity that ends in pregnancy or destroys marriages, for instance. Why win in life and lose out in the victory celebration? There is a right way and a wrong way to enjoy being a winner.

Joseph knew that sleeping with the boss's wife was the wrong way to celebrate being big man on campus (head of Potiphar's household), not just because of who he was, but because of who he served on this earth and in heaven. He knew that first and foremost he served the King of kings and Lord of lords, God Almighty, who was ultimately his source for winning against all odds and, the Bible says, he refused the advances of Potiphar's wife.

"No one is greater in this house than I am. My master has withheld nothing from me except you, because you are his wife. How then

could I do such a wicked thing and sin against God?" And though she spoke to Joseph day after day, he refused to go to bed with her or even be with her.

Genesis 39:9–10 NIV

Day after day this woman offered herself to Joseph, perhaps in some warped way thinking of it as his reward for being so handsome and such a good-looking winner. A lot of people would have yielded to the very first temptation of wrong, justifying it as something they deserve to have because of who they've become as a winner—the team captain or the star of the show or the president of the company or the pastor of a church, or the person with all the money, the one others have to answer to. The truth is, if we don't do this celebrating right, what we really are is the loser!

How relentless will you be to live right?

Why do anything to lose, including messing up the win in the victory celebration? Why get to the finish line just to stumble and fall? In God's way of seeing things, the victory is just an open door for Him.

Do the Right Thing

*Let your light so shine before men, that they may see your good works, and **glorify your Father** which is in heaven.*

Matthew 5:16 KJV

It is important how you celebrate so that you glorify God in all you do. People can see the good works God has blessed you with. You appear as a winner in their eyes so you have no right to do wrong because they see that too, and it does not bring glory to

God. Being a winner did not give Joseph a right to sin and have a sexual relationship with someone else's wife, because it is a sin according to God.

This is an interesting part of winning. Many people only want to go along with the God process until they win in life. Then they feel that they don't need any further use of God or the process wrapped in faith. It is as though God does not know how to help the celebrator. Yet we are not meant to begin with God and then stop when we become a winner.

Joseph did not give in to this way of thinking. He said, "How then could I do such a wicked thing and sin against God?" When he became successful, he still acknowledged God, remembering that God was in his life. He understood that even though Pharaoh's captain may have hired him and that he actually worked for Potiphar in his house, God still had the final authority in the matters of his life. He further understood that if he was to continue to have God's winning ways in his life, he needed to please God, not himself or others.

Perhaps Potiphar would have never found out about the illicit affair between Joseph and his wife. It could have been a one-night stand with her, but to Joseph *God would have seen and known,* and that was enough for him to say no to her and become a total winner—even over all odds against the pleasures of sin for a season. (See Heb. 11:25.)

God knows what you are dealing with in your life; that is why you can ask Him to help you. Even right now, you can call on Him and He said He will answer you. (See Jer. 33:3.)

As we continue to read the account of Joseph's life in the book of Genesis, it seems that he made a very bad mistake by not participating with evil and that his decision to stay away from the illicit sexual affair with a married woman was the wrong choice. Yet Potiphar's wife actually set Joseph up for failure because he would not commit sin with her.

That woman was relentless and she pulled at Joseph's clothes as she begged for his affection. In the process of Joseph fleeing her attempted seduction, she caught ahold of his coat. She used that coat to make up a lie to her husband that Joseph had tried to rape her and had left his coat as he fled. When Potiphar heard of this, he was furious at Joseph and ended up sentencing him to spend several years in Pharaoh's dungeon. (See Gen. 39:19–20.)

Can you imagine doing the right thing in the eyes of God and yet being sentenced to jail anyway?

So there Joseph was back in a pit again. What a loser, right? Absolutely wrong. When God is with you, it does not matter who is against you or where you end up. You still win in the end!

The Lord was with Joseph there, too, and he granted Joseph favor with the chief jailer. Before long, the jailer put Joseph in charge of all the other prisoners and over everything that happened in the prison. The chief jailer had no more worries after that, because Joseph took care of everything.

Genesis 39:21–23 NLT

Joseph was living proof again that if your life has been filled with lemons, God will help you make it into lemonade, because God is your Helper. While Joseph was in prison, though, the fact that God does allow future events to be revealed became much more evident.

A Glimpse of Things to Come

After Joseph was overseer of the prison for some time, two men from the king's staff were imprisoned in Joseph's jail. (See Gen. 40.) One night they each had a dream and were troubled by their meaning, but they did not know of anyone in prison who could interpret their dreams and tell them their future. There were no astrologers, witches, or mediums (the type of people sought after in Egypt for such things at that time) who, in an evil way, could give them the message about their future.

When Joseph heard about the need for the interpretation of their dreams he replied, "Do not interpretations belong to God? Tell them [the dreams] to me, please" (v. 8). Notice he did not say interpretations belong to the soothsayer or the witchcraft worker or the medium channeler or any other wicked way of hearing the future—whether one's life holds a future of winning or losing. He said that interpreting the future belongs to God, and he proceeded to interpret the two men's dreams.

The butler's dream meant that within three days he would be released from jail and be serving Pharaoh again. The baker wasn't so fortunate. His dream meant he would be delivered up from the jail only to be beheaded and have the birds eat his carcass. A sad fate, but a true interpretation, and both came to pass just as God had revealed to the man of God that they would.

I believe this is profound—not only to know that God holds the future in His hands for us and will bring us to our future in a blessed way, but that He also will reveal to us our future, if we will enquire of Him. He may not reveal it when or in the way we expect, but He will give us a glimpse of things to come if we seek Him faithfully. Here's something else that is profound about this. The gift of interpreting dreams that God had given to Joseph had a great influence in the lives of those who did not even know his God.

Although Joseph had told the butler to remember him when he got out of jail, the man forgot him (Gen. 40:14,23), leaving him still in what would appear to be a losing position—in jail, though the overseer of the jail house. But God knew where Joseph was every moment. In fact, I want you to stop reading for a minute and meditate (or think) on this thought:

> God knows where you are right now. He knows if you are winning in life or losing in life. Neither your present condition or your future before you is foreign to God. Even though God knows where you are, He will not just leave you there if you stay faithful to His ways.

Every person has a plan that God has already worked out for them to win in life. For Joseph this gift of interpreting future events and dreams by way of the help of God's Spirit was part of God's plan for him—and it was about to prove to be of world-wide importance to the entire known human race during Joseph's lifetime.

Making the Winning Deposit

It literally took two more years in prison before Joseph's gift resurfaced in importance to those around him. This time Pharaoh had a dream that was delivered to him from God regarding the future events about the mighty and prosperous nation of Egypt. (See Gen. 40:1.) The need for an interpreter of dreams was in the forefront of society again, and Joseph would be brought to center stage because he was faithful to God and was patient, even in the midst of imprisonment due to false accusations years before.

Always remember that if you are born to win (born again), you will never be held back from what God has for you ultimately if you do things God's way. Let's look at this further.

Pharaoh had a very complex dream regarding the future of the entire nation of Egypt and the surrounding nations. (See Gen. 41:1-7.) This recurring dream greatly troubled him, but none of the magicians or wise men of his court could interpret it.

> *Then spake the chief butler unto Pharaoh, saying, I do remember my faults this day.*
>
> Genesis 41:9 KJV

I believe this is a profound key to remember. The chief butler took responsibility for his fault of overlooking a seeming loser (in the eyes of society) in jail himself (falsely), who had an ability to interpret dreams because he had a relationship with God. (The butler didn't know that Joseph's gift could eventually help to save an entire nation.) It is very interesting to me how God packages gifts in people. He endows them with gifts on the inside, but He doesn't always make the outside appealing with striking wrapping for us to see.

Some very unassuming people have made some of the most profound contributions to help mankind in our history. Such was the case for Joseph, a foreigner, someone of another nationality who had to learn the language, customs, and values of the nation of Egypt. To all outward appearances it seemed as if he certainly would not know anything that could help such an advanced and wealthy people as the leaders of almighty Egypt. Yet there sitting in jail was a winner with the ability to answer what only God could answer through a man.

It was not Joseph's fault that he was not taken seriously; it was the butler's fault and at least he did admit it. His fault was not remembering Joseph, which could have been detrimental to all the residents and neighboring nations close to Egypt. What this young man who was in jail had inside of him was enough to save thousands of people from death.

Perhaps while you are reading this book you may have inside of you the key to some great mystery, like how to cure one of the world's most deadly diseases. It would be to the advantage of the entire human race that the formula for winning in medicine (or any other field) be taken seriously in your life.

I believe God gives us every answer to this world's problems in the lives of people. Everyone has a winning contribution to leave in this planet, including you. It is actually our fault if we (as human beings) do not help you to bring it out for all to enjoy and benefit from. That is why it is so important that you are reading this book.

I pray that you will be inspired to make the winning deposit that God has placed in you and that He will bring people across your path who will help to lift you up to the place of prominence to make your contribution to mankind. The butler was brought across Joseph's path by God and was instrumental in helping in that way. Let's see what happened as a result.

Pharaoh had given way to hearing from the evil side of interpretations of the future to no avail. He didn't know there was another side he could hear from. It is so important to know that there are only two sides to revealing the future—either God through good means, or the devil (Lucifer) through evil means. According to the Bible, that includes witchcraft, magicians, sorcerers, the occult, divination, fortune telling, horoscopes, stargazing, séances, and many other forms of evil that delve into revealing the future.

Pharaoh needed some real answers to some real concerns about the future of all the people of his nation, and he wasn't going to get those answers from rabbits coming out of hats or faces appearing in a crystal ball. Lady luck could not do the job for him. With the urgency he felt on the inside regarding this dream, he had to have some answers quick—and they had to be the right answers, not just any answer. We can see this again and again in the Bible where the serious answers for life came only from the God of the Bible.

You may be a winner, but it may not be your fault that you have not been taken seriously as a winner. Just stay faithful and use your faith and patience, and you can inherit the promises God has for you. God knows how to expose the gifts and abilities He has given you, just as He did for Joseph.

How did this ability of God in Joseph bring him from the pit to the palace? When the butler spoke to Pharaoh about Joseph having the answers he needed, Pharaoh sent for Joseph, and he was quickly taken to the palace from the dungeon after he had shaved and changed his clothes. (See Gen. 41:9-14.)

Joseph may not have looked like a winner (he looked like a prisoner and a loser), but it was not what was on the outside that mattered; it was what was on the inside that mattered. You may not look like you are a winner outwardly, but you are definitely a winner on the inside if you are born again and following after God. It takes but a moment to change the outside as we can see here, but only God can change the inside of you. If you haven't already, let Him do it now.

From the Pit to the Palace

As Joseph stood before Pharaoh, he told Joseph about his dream and asked him to interpret it, but Joseph said, "I cannot do it...but God will give Pharaoh the answer he desires" (Gen. 41:16 NIV). This man Joseph would not take the credit for being able to do what no one else could do. He said the God of the Bible would give Pharaoh the answer he needed. Notice he didn't say anything about selling it to him for a fortune-teller's session price, but that God would give freely to Pharaoh the answer he desired.

So Pharaoh told Joseph his dream and finished by saying, "I told this to the magicians, but none could explain it to me" (v. 24). Please see this. Magicians, soothsayers, or fortune-tellers may say some things that have a semblance of truth due to the fact that they are attempting to conjure up from the spiritual realm answers from other sources, but that method displeases God and is evil.

God gives real and deep answers to complex questions without charge—though there is a "price" to pay. The price is the cost of living a godly lifestyle according to His Word.

Joseph had proven that he would and could do that very well, even though he appeared to be a loser, and he proceeded to interpret Pharaoh's dreams. After he told Pharaoh the meaning was seven years of plenty followed by seven years of famine, he finished by saying, "The reason the dream was given to Pharaoh in two forms is that the matter has been firmly decided by God, and God will do it soon" (v. 32 NIV). Then Joseph suggested that

Pharaoh appoint someone over the land to oversee and store up the harvest during the plentiful years to be used in the seven years of famine.

Notice that Joseph had begun to allow not only the gift of the interpretation of dreams to be revealed through him, but also his wise counsel (which comes from God), along with his leadership ability. Pharaoh liked the idea and said, "Can we find anyone like this man, one in whom is the spirit of God?" (v. 38 NIV). Pharaoh saw in Joseph someone who could help him to handle government leadership and governmental planning and prudence in a very political and polarized society, but he saw something else too.

Isn't it profound that a governmental leader who was foreign to Joseph's God would be able to sense in Joseph the Spirit of God based on his simple advice of a few words? Pharaoh recognized that the Spirit of God in Joseph was not in anyone else, making Joseph very unique—not like the magicians and other false prophets, but someone who they apparently had been looking for to help them out.

People are looking for true winners, but the only real winners are those who have God as their winning source. They may not know what they are really looking for at first, but they will know when those kinds of people show up—and I believe that you are one of those winners too!

What Pharaoh saw in Joseph made him promote Joseph to second in command of all Egypt. Joseph was also given a prominent wife, "robes of fine linen," gold jewelry, and his own chariot to ride in. (Gen. 41:39-46.) At this point there was no doubt who Joseph was—he was dressed like a winner, he rode like a winner, he lived like a winner, he was related to winners, and he led like a winner. When did he first become a winner? Long before he interpreted Pharaoh's dreams.

Joseph was a winner when God first met him (when as a young boy, Joseph chose to follow God), and He made him to be a winner. The butcher, the baker, and Pharaoh discovered only what Joseph already was. They did not make Joseph a winner; they only recognized the obvious—*if the God of the Bible is with you, you are a winner.* Circumstances, challenges, setbacks, living in the pits or plots of the enemy cannot keep you from your destiny. If you remain faithful to God, you will manifest into what God has created you to be—and it will be obvious for everyone to see.

Joseph went on leading as a winner, never again to be thrown in the pits of life, and his winning ways included restored relationships with his brothers. They ended up in the midst of the famine Joseph had foreseen for Pharaoh, and they went to Egypt looking for food for their families' survival at the direction of their father at home. Unbeknown to them their own brother ruled as the second in leadership of the nation.

At first they did not recognize Joseph as their own blood brother because the winning ways of his obedience to God's purpose for his life had transformed both his station in life and his physical appearance—but Joseph recognized his brothers. Even though they had thrown him in the first pit of his life, in the trek to success while he was a young teen, he longed to let them know that he was still alive and that God had made him this awesome winner and placed him in the position of prime minister of Egypt.

Can you see now why Joseph is a great example of what God can do with you if you will apply His principles (covered in this book) to your life? God's anointing on Joseph to win changed the nation of Egypt and the surrounding nations and caused him to be in a strong leadership position. It also changed his family and brought them eventually into the land of plenty called the land of Goshen. (See Gen. 47:5–6.)

Because Joseph became a winner with the God of the Bible, he became a winner in all other areas of life including wisdom, knowledge, family, health, and wealth as he used the gift that God had given him. Joseph continued in success to the point of controlling the economic commerce of all the nations in the area during his lifetime. In fact, he ended up controlling all the wealth in the land. (See Gen. 47:13-25.) That sounds like a man winning against all odds.

His life even ended like a winner.

[Joseph] lived a hundred and ten years and saw the third generation of Ephraim's children. Also the children of Makir son of Manasseh were placed at birth on Joseph's knees. Then Joseph said to his brothers, "I am about to die. But God will surely come to your aid and take you up out of this land to the land he promised on oath to Abraham, Isaac and Jacob." And Joseph made the sons of Israel swear an oath and said, "...then you must carry my bones up from this place." So Joseph died at the age of a hundred and ten.

Genesis 50:22-26 NIV

What a way to win against all odds! The good new is that God's way of winning works for anyone who will allow His Spirit to work through them.

Conclusion

This book was written to teach you how to win against all odds in life, assist in giving you endurance and encouragement, and help you to have hope that what you read is possible to come to pass in your life. Joseph's life was an extraordinary example of what I have presented in these pages—winners relying on God for their future success. Yet the Bible tells about many other godly winners similar to Joseph.

Again and again in the Scriptures we see that God is glorified when people use His processes through His promises in His Word to win against all odds. The Word of God speaks of David, who defeated the giant Goliath against all odds. (See 1 Sam. 17:50.) First Kings 3:5-15 talks about Solomon winning, with one dream, riches and honor and wisdom. In the book of Daniel, we find another man (Daniel) who decided to win against all odds using the methods God displays throughout the Bible.

Joseph, Mary's espoused husband, was led by dreams of where to go with their newborn babe called Jesus. The Word of God speaks of Abraham (formerly Abram), and later Paul (once known as Saul) being direct by dreams and visions, and the same thing happened to many of the other apostles. The awesome Spirit of the living God led them to victory by dreams and visions, along with so very many others who simply put God's promises into their processes of winning against all odds.

Throughout the Bible we see this same pattern of a true winner against the worst of odds:

- Have a relationship with God.

- Use that relationship to benefit those you serve.

- Even in tough times do not fear what man can do to you, and stay faithful.

- Once you have the victory and get out of the pits of life, give God all the praise for you being a winner again.

If God can do it for these and others thousands of years ago who chose to follow this pattern, He is the same yesterday, today, and forever, and He can do it for you now in your area of expertise. This is not ego, pride, arrogance, pretense, or fantasy—this is truth from God's Word.

Everything that was written in the past was written to teach us, so that through endurance and the encouragement of the Scriptures we might have hope.

Romans 15:4 NIV

Allow the Scriptures to do this for you, no matter what the matter is with you. Use this way of winning against *every* matter—business, science, health, family, finances, or relationship matters, government, social, technical, or even sexual matters. Whatever the matter is, God's wisdom and understanding excels. Joseph and other winners in the Bible were just common people with something special that God had given them to help them to excel past those of their time.

It is important to note that the skills and abilities (of people in the Bible) that are being mentioned here are not just religious or spiritual skills but skills in leadership, government, business, and people skills. What am I saying? Just because the source is spiritual in nature—the Spirit of God being the source of the insight, skills, or revelation of visions and dreams—the outcome and results can affect nations, people, resources, money, and the thinking process regarding hard matters that affect all physical aspects of society. In other words, their knowledge was not just for church-related things!

Joseph was not doing a Sunday school Bible quiz when he faced Pharaoh in the palace. This was about matters that mattered to a worldly, not God-fearing, ruler of a ruthless nation that had conquered many other nations and peoples. In that area is where Joseph excelled in the matter of their future existence above all the other non-foreign advisors and pseudo-religious people in Pharaoh's court.

At this point I want you to expand your thinking even more. This may seem like an egotistical thing to do, but you must see yourself as better in knowledge, wisdom, and matters that matter to your station in life than those who have not the God of the Bible in their life. Remember, we've learned that *as a man thinks in his heart, so is he.* (See Prov. 23:7.)

I have listed in this book many great principles like that one for you to use. Let's see what you've learned and is important to remember as you are being transformed into a winner.

1. In every human being there is a desire to win. You have a strong desire to win in life, just like a newborn baby desires milk from the mother.

2. Once you are connected to God, you become a born winner.

3. You will need to talk as a winner. From now on you should use only winning words—no more words of defeat. You are a winner, so talk like one.

4. What you believe is vitally important. Take heed to what you hear, see, and read.

5. Learn to think as a winner. Your thoughts are very important. Your mind is like a computer; program only good things into it.

6. Learn to hear as a winner. Pay special attention to what comes into your ears; sort out the good from the bad.

7. Live your life as a winner. Hold your head up; keep going forward, having purpose in everything you do.

8. You will live according to the way you think. Your world is created by your thoughts. If you think you can, you will.

9. Faith is used to bring things you desire from an unseen world into the seen world. Faith is the "sixth sense."

10. Faith speaks. If you believe you have what you desire, then you will say it.

11. Faith can and will move big problems. We have all been faced with a problem, but how you face it—with faith— is what's important. You are not alone; thousands of other people have experienced the same thing. Face your problems and any fears.

12. You must speak words full of power. Talk big. Sometimes I like to say to talk big and "bad" (a slang word that means good) as long as you can. Talk the good that you desire until you live the life you really want.

13. You must first see it inside of you before you see it outside of you.

14. Prayer is important—and you have the tools to now succeed.

15. Your vision is only a wish if not written down. Write it down and make it plain; wait for it; it will come.

16. When you receive the answer, praise and acknowledge God, as He is your source of winning in this life. Include in your cadre of success arsenal the requirement to give God praise for being your source of God-given processes leading to victory.

These proven principles will take you from losing ways to a winning life. I encourage you to use all that you have learned in this book, all the while being strong and of good courage and unafraid, for God is with you wherever you go. With Him, you can win against all odds!

Prayer of Salvation

God loves you—no matter who you are, no matter what your past. God loves you so much that He gave His one and only begotten Son for you. The Bible tells us that "...whoever believes in him shall not perish but have eternal life" (John 3:16 NIV). Jesus laid down His life and rose again so that we could spend eternity with Him in heaven and experience His absolute best on earth. If you would like to receive Jesus into your life, say the following prayer out loud and mean it from your heart:

Heavenly Father, I come to You admitting that I am a sinner. Right now, I choose to turn away from sin, and I ask You to cleanse me of all unrighteousness. I believe that Your Son, Jesus, died on the cross to take away my sins. I also believe that He rose again from the dead so that I might be forgiven of my sins and made righteous through faith in Him. I call upon the name of Jesus Christ to be the Savior and Lord of my life. Jesus, I choose to follow You and ask that You fill me with the power of the Holy Spirit. I declare that right now I am a child of God. I am free from sin and full of the righteousness of God. I am saved in Jesus' name. Amen.

If you prayed this prayer to receive Jesus Christ as your Savior for the first time, please contact us on the web at **www.harrison-house.com** to receive a free book.

Or you may write to us at

Harrison House
P.O. Box 35035
Tulsa, Oklahoma 74153

Endnotes

Chapter 1

1 Robert Jamieson, A. R. Fausset, and David Brown, *Jamieson, Fausset, Brown Commentary Critical and Explanatory on the Whole Bible*, "Commentary on Colossians 2," available from http://www.studylight.org/com/jfb/view.cgi?book= col&chapter=002, Colossians 2:9.

2 Thayer and Smith, *The KJV New Testament Greek Lexicon*, "Greek Lexicon entry for Pas," available from http://www.biblestudytools.net/Lexicons/Greek/grk.cgi? number=3956&version=kjv, s.v. "whatsoever," 1 John 5:4.

Chapter 2

1 Matthew Henry, *Matthew Henry's Complete Commentary on the Whole Bible*, "Commentary on Hebrews 4," available from http://bible.crosswalk.com/ Commentaries/MatthewHenryComplete/mhc-com.cgi?book=heb&chapter=004, s.v. "Verses 11-16."

2 *Merriam-Webster's Collegiate Dictionary*, 11 ed. (Springfield, Massachusetts: Merriam-Webster, Inc., 2003), s.v. "meditate."

3 Ibid., s.v. "ponder."

4 Based on a definition from Brown, Driver, Briggs and Gesenius, *The KJV Old Testament Hebrew Lexicon,* "Hebrew Lexicon entry for Raga`," available from http://www.biblestudytools.net/Lexicons/Hebrew/heb.cgi?number=7280&version =kjv, s.v. "moment."

5 Ibid., "Hebrew Lexicon entry for Rega`," available from http://www.biblestudy-tools.net/Lexicons/Hebrew/heb.cgi?number=7281&version=kjv, s.v. "moment."

Chapter 3

1 Thayer and Smith, "Greek Lexicon entry for Pneuma," available from http://www.biblestudytools.net/Lexicons/Greek/grk.cgi?number=4151&version= kjv, s.v. "spirit," 1 Thessalonians 5:23.

2 Based on information from Albert Barnes, *Barnes' Notes on the New Testament*, "Commentary on 1 Thessalonians 5," available from http://www.studylight.org/ com/bnn/view.cgi?book=1th&chapter=005, s.v. "Verse 23."

3 Ibid., "Commentary on Hebrews 4:12" available from http://www.studylight.org/ com/bnn/view.cgi?book=heb&chapter=004, s.v. "Verse 12."

4 Based on information from Albert Barnes, "Commentary on 1 Thessalonians 5," available from http://www.studylight.org/com/bnn/view.cgi?book=1th&chapter= 005, s.v. "Verse 23."

[5] Based on information from Robert Jamieson, A. R. Fausset, and David Brown, *Jamieson, Fausset, Brown Commentary Critical and Explanatory on the Whole Bible*, "Commentary on Hebrews 4," available from http://www.studylight.org/com/jfb/view.cgi?book=heb&chapter=004, s.v. "even to the dividing asunder of soul and spirit," Hebrews 4:1-16.

[6] Based on information from John Gill, *The New John Gill Exposition of the Entire Bible*, "Commentary on Jude 1:20," available from http://www.studylight.org/com/geb/view.cgi?book=jude&chapter=001&verse=020, s.v. "praying in the Holy Ghost."

[7] God anoints us by giving us His Holy Spirit (when we are born again and ask God to fill us with His Spirit); His anointing is the power of His Spirit in us and on us to help us do those things we can't do on our own. Based on information from John Gill, "Commentary on Acts 10:38," available from http://www.studylight.org/com/geb/view.cgi?book=ac&chapter=010&verse=038, s.v. "the Holy Ghost and with power."

[8] Ibid., available from http://www.studylight.org/com/geb/view.cgi?book=isa&chapter=061&verse=002, s.v. "To proclaim the acceptable year of the Lord," Isaiah 61.2.

[9] Albert Barnes, available from http://www.e-sword.net/commentaries.html, s.v. "To proclaim the acceptable year of the Lord," Isaiah 61:2.

[10] Based on information from Albert Barnes, available from http://www.e-sword.net/commentaries.html, s.v. "The double," Isaiah 61:7.

[11] John Gill, "Commentary on Luke 4:18", available from http://www.studylight.org/com/geb/view.cgi?book=lu&chapter=004&verse=018, s.v. "To preach the Gospel to the poor."

[12] Albert Barnes, available from http://www.studylight.org/com/bnn/view.cgi?book=lu&chapter=004, s.v. "Deliverance to the captives."

[13] *Keil & Delitzsch Commentary on the Old Testament*, available from http://www.e-sword.net/commentaries.html, s.v. "Numbers 27:15-17."

Chapter 4

[1] Thayer and Smith, "Greek Lexicon entry for Kardia," available from http://www.biblestudytools.net/Lexicons/Greek/grk.cgi?number=2588&version=kjv, s.v. "kardia."

[2] Ibid., "Greek Lexicon entry for Anakainoo," available from http://www.biblestudytools.net/Lexicons/Greek/grk.cgi?number=341&version=kjv, s.v. "renew."

[3] Ibid., "Greek Lexicon entry for Anakainizo," available from http://www.biblestudytools.net/Lexicons/Greek/grk.cgi?number=340&version=kjv, s.v. "renew."

[4] Based on definitions from Merriam-Webster, s.v. "how."

Chapter 5

[1] Thayer and Smith, *The KJV New Testament Greek Lexicon,* "Greek Lexicon entry for Pistis," available from http://www.biblestudytools.net/Lexicons/Greek/grk.cgi?number=4102&version=kjv, s.v. "faith," Hebrews 11:1.

[2] Based on information from Thayer and Smith, "Greek Lexicon entry for Hupostasis," available from http://www.biblestudytools.net/Lexicons/Greek/grk.cgi?number=5287&version=kjv, s.v. "substance," Hebrews 11:1.

[3] Barton W. Johnson, *People's New Testament,* "Commentary on Hebrews 11," available from http://bible.crosswalk.com/Commentaries/PeoplesNewTestament/pnt.cgi?book=heb&chapter=011, s.v. "1-3. Faith is the substance," Hebrews 11:1.

[4] Jamieson, Fausset, and Brown, "Commentary on Hebrews 11," available from http://www.studylight.org/com/jfb/view.cgi?book=heb&chapter=011, s.v. "evidence," Hebrews 11:1.

[5] Ibid.

[6] Ibid., available from http://www.studylight.org/com/jfb/view.cgi?book=1jo&chapter=005, s.v. "this is the victory that overcometh," 1 John 5:4.

[7] Based on information from Albert Barnes, s.v. "Even our faith," 1 John 5:4.

Chapter 6

[1] Based on information from Thayer and Smith, "Greek Lexicon entry for Opheilema," available from http://www.biblestudytools.net/Lexicons/Greek/grk.cgi?number=3783&version=kjv, s.v. "debt," Matthew 6:12.

Chapter 7

[1] These three points are based on information from Matthew Henry, *Matthew Henry's Complete Commentary on the Whole Bible,* available from http://bible.crosswalk.com/Commentaries/MatthewHenryComplete/mhc-com.cgi?book=hab&chapter=002, Habakkuk 2:1-4.

[2] *Noah Webster's Dictionary of American English,* available from http://www.e-sword.net/dictionaries.html, s.v. "wait."

Chapter 8

[1] Matthew Henry, available from http://bible.crosswalk.com/Commentaries/MatthewHenryComplete/mhc-com.cgi?book=heb&chapter=005, s.v. "Verses 10-14," Hebrews 5.

[2] Ibid.

Chapter 9

[1] Brown, Driver, Briggs and Gesenius, "Hebrew Lexicon entry for Tavah, available from http://www.biblestudytools.net/Lexicons/Hebrew/heb.cgi?number=8428& version=kjv, s.v. "grieve," Psalm 78:41.

[2] Thayer and Smith, "Greek Lexicon entry for Christos," available from http://www.biblestudytools.net/Lexicons/Greek/grk.cgi?number=5547&version= kjv, s.v. "Christ," Matthew 1:16.

Chapter 10

[1] Matthew Henry, "Commentary on Luke 4," available from http://bible.cross-walk.com/Commentaries/MatthewHenryComplete/mhc-com.cgi?book= lu&chapter=004, Luke 4:1-13.

[2] Albert Barnes, *Barnes' Notes on the New Testament*, "Commentary on Ephesians 6," available from http://www.studylight.org/com/bnn/view.cgi?book=eph&chapter= 006, s.v. "Verse 14."

[3] John Darby, *John Darby's Synopsis of the New Testament*, "Commentary on Ephesians 6, available from <http://bible.crosswalk.com/Commentaries/DarbysSynopsisof NewTestament/dby.cgi?book=eph&chapter=006>, s.v. "Ephesians 6:16."

[4] Based on a definition from Brown, Driver, Briggs and Gesenius, "Hebrew Lexicon entry for Tsalach," available from <http://www.biblestudytools.net/Lexicons/ Hebrew/heb.cgi?number=6743&version=kjv>. s.v. "prosper," Isaiah 54:17.

[5] Adam Clarke, "Commentary on Ephesians 6," available from http://www.study-light.org/com/acc/view.cgi?book=eph&chapter=006, s.v. "The sword of the Spirit," Ephesians 6:17.

[6] Albert Barnes, "Commentary on Ephesians 6," available from http://www.study-light.org/com/bnn/view.cgi?book=eph&chapter=006, s.v. "Verse 18."

About the Author

Dr. Shorter is the pastor and founder of Pacific Christian Center Church, a vibrant, growing, nondenominational church in Tacoma, Washington. Leaving his successful secular radio and television broadcasting career as a television host on the Seattle, Washington, ABC affiliates, Dr. Donald Shorter Sr. founded Pacific Christian Center Church in January of 1987 with his family of four as the only members. Construction on their new state-of-the-art worship center was completed in August 2002, and the church has expanded to several locations in Washington State.

Dr. Shorter received his masters in business administration in 1993, and his doctorate of ministry in 1999. He is presently completing his PhD. Dr. Shorter is an instrument and multi-engine aircraft pilot of both airplanes and helicopters and is affectionately known as "The Flying Pastor." He regularly pilots various aircraft to services each week.

He has served on numerous boards throughout the past 15 years as well as currently serving on the board of directors of the Fellowship of Inner-City Word of Faith Ministries, a worldwide pastors and ministers accountability organization. It is under this organization that he served as the region one director, which comprised fellowship churches in the states of Washington, Oregon, Alaska, and areas of Northern California.

Dr. Shorter met the former Kathy Lynette Hill while attending Clover Park High School in Lakewood, Washington. They were married in July of 1974 and have three children.

Today, he and his wife minister the word of faith through Pacific Christian Center Church's worldwide ministry. They minister to thousands each week through their speaking engagements, radio and television teaching broadcasts, regular church services, and business seminars.

Their ministry accomplishments have touched many segments of our society through their faith-based outreaches such as Real Dads in America, Kathi's Kids Outreach, Excellence in Business, as well as the Men of Excellence, Women of Wealth, the Fat Free Lifestyle, and First Lady's Boutique, a women's retraining and career clothing outreach.

Dr. Donald and Kathy Shorter are best known for teaching the Word of God in a practical, powerful, straightforward way, causing lifestyles to be miraculously changed through the ministry of the Word. Through their numerous books, such as *Take Control of your Thoughts, The Power in You, Guard Your Heart,* and *Living in the Kingdom of God,* along with their regular television broadcasts, videotapes, seminars, CDs and cassettes, they are helping to changes lives throughout North America, Europe, Africa, and around the world.

To contact Dr. Donald Shorter,
write to:
Dr. Donald Shorter
P.O. Box 44800
Tacoma, WA 98448
Or to:
Pacific Christian Center Church
3211 112th Street East
Tacoma, WA 98446
(235)536-0801

Or visit him on the Web at:
www.pacificchristiancenter.org

*Please include your prayer requests
and comments when you write.*

Other Books by Dr. Donald Shorter

Take Control of Your Thoughts

Casting Down Imaginations

The Power in You

Books by Kathy Shorter

Desperate Dieters

Guard Your Heart

Heaven Yes! Hell No!

Living in the Kingdom of God

Coming Out of Egypt

Additional copies of this book are available at fine bookstores
everywhere or from **www.harrisonhouse.com**.

The Harrison House Vision

Proclaiming the truth and the power
Of the Gospel of Jesus Christ
With excellence;

Challenging Christians to
Live victoriously,
Grow spiritually,
Know God intimately.